PUBLIC RELATIONS ETHICS

PUBLIC
RELATIONS
ETHICS

PHILIP SEIB

KATHY FITZPATRICK

HARCOURT BRACE COLLEGE PUBLISHERS
Fort Worth   Philadelphia   San Diego
New York   Orlando   Austin   San Antonio
Toronto   Montreal   London   Sydney   Tokyo

HM
263
.S418
1995

Publisher Ted Buchholz
Senior Acquisitions Editor Stephen Jordan
Project Editor John Haakenson
Production Manager Tad Gaither
Senior Art Director Don Fujimoto
Editorial Assistant Margaret McAndrew Beasley

Cover Image: "Slate" *Phototone Vol. 1* © Letraset

ISBN: 0-15-5019430

Library of Congress Catalog Card Number: 94-77555

Address for Editorial Correspondence: Harcourt Brace College Publishers, 301 Commerce Street, Suite 3700, Fort Worth, TX 76102.

Address for Orders: Harcourt Brace & Company, 6277 Sea Harbor Drive, Orlando, FL 32887-6777. 1-800-782-4479, or 1-800-433-0001 (in Florida).

Printed in the United States of America

4 5 6 7 8 9 0 1 2 3 039 9 8 7 6 5 4 3 2 1

Preface

"**E**thical public relations" is often scoffed at as an oxymoron. This is a bad rap.

The vast majority of public relations practitioners consider themselves members of an honorable profession with obligations to the public as well as to their clients. Recognizing the pervasiveness and influence of public relations messages, these men and women try to match their power with commensurately ethical behavior.

They have done so with remarkably little academic support. Ethical issues often receive minimal attention in public relations textbooks and classrooms. This book breaks new ground by being devoted exclusively to ethics and by presenting diverse theories and cases to be taught and contemplated.

Designed to be used in introductory public relations, mass media, or communication ethics courses, *Public Relations Ethics* exists primarily to raise ethical consciousness—to make ethics more comprehensible to both students and practitioners of public relations. Its discussions of principles and its examples are also designed to help those who interact with public relations professionals understand the functions and duties of this field.

Running throughout the book is the theme of moral responsibility: the need for the individual practitioner and the industry to evaluate thoughtfully the means used to reach objectives and the consequences of exercising public relations power.

Chapter one examines the importance of professionalism. Negative images cast their shadow on public relations work, underscoring this industry's need to improve its own public relations. At issue are the endorsement of consistent standards of professional conduct and practitioners' personal commitment to ethical principles. The link between an individual's ethical behavior and the professionalism of the entire field is unbreakable.

Chapter two addresses the need for a systematic approach to ethical decision making in public relations. Public relations professionals have diverse allegiances. When faced with potentially conflicting loyalties, which should take precedence?

Diverse influences shape answers to such questions:

- legal requirements (or absence of such pressures)
- client policies and expectations
- codified standards of the public relations industry and of the individual public relations firm/department/practitioner
- personal values

Chapter three analyzes some theories of ethics—the intellectual foundations on which professional standards are developed. Moral philosophy has both academic and practical facets, all of which are helpful when making decisions about public relations policy and practice. The standard answer to most questions about ethics begins with, "It depends." That beginning and the situational ethics that follow are logical responses to daily ethical challenges. But practicality should be grounded in solid principles.

Chapter four looks at fundamental business practices—getting and keeping clients and serving client organizations. What level of competency should be guaranteed and what results should be promised? What special considerations come into play when dealing with a controversial client? What rules should govern competition within the public relations industry? Should special standards be devised for work in foreign cultures?

Chapter five examines the elusiveness of truth. Just defining "truth" can be difficult. Some people are absolutists; others let truth be shaped by varying degrees of expediency. Sometimes telling "the whole truth" is replaced by telling "selective truths" that are accurate in themselves but constitute less than the complete story.

Problems arise when the teller of the "truth" and the audience for that "truth" have different standards. For instance, puffery may seem harmless exaggeration to some, while it is seen as deception by others. The border between the two is sometimes blurred, but ethical public relations professionals must not stray across it. Ground rules about such matters should be thoughtfully considered before disseminating information on which people will rely.

Chapter six examines a relationship that is both symbiotic and adversarial—the links between public relations and journalism. Inextricably tied by their responsibilities as purveyors of information, the professionals in each field should possess a thorough understanding of the other's techniques and standards. Just as public relations practitioners should be expected to emphasize the best attributes of their clients, so, too, should journalists be expected to evaluate and investigate those representations before passing them on to *their* clients—the news consumers.

Most journalists understand and expect the dynamic tension that exists when public relations practitioners are advancing their causes or clients. But journalists also expect a certain respect to be shown toward their profession. A public relations effort is headed for trouble when it is based on a strategy that is—or is even perceived as—denigrating toward journalists as ethical professionals. Tactics such as offering free trips to cover events might win some friends, but can also prove counterproductive.

Interaction between the two professions is constant, and it should be governed by a carefully thought-out professional etiquette based on mutual respect.

Chapter seven addresses some of the most visible issues with which the public relations industry must grapple: those arising in political campaigns, work for governmental clients, lobbying, and litigation support. These are areas in which passions often run high. As consultants to candidates or as champions of institutions and causes, public relations practitioners may find themselves hailed by partisans on the side they're on while being vilified by those on the other.

When involved in political or quasi-political work, public relations professionals must realize how difficult it can be to observe the line between advocacy and tampering with the political process. Truth is often a scarce commodity in these arenas; ethical public relations practitioners can help change that.

Public relations crises are the focus of chapter eight. High stakes, high visibility, and high pressure combine to challenge the skills and ethics of practitioners. While the temptations of the quick (but not always honest) fix are great, these occasions also provide a chance to validate an important maxim: ethical public relations is good business. Looking principally at the Tylenol poisonings of 1982 and 1986 and the Exxon Valdez oil spill of 1989, this chapter examines lessons to be learned from successful and unsuccessful public relations responses to crises.

In public relations, as in other professions, ethical standards are never static; they evolve apace with business practices. Chapter nine evaluates the profession's status and its prospects—how this field is likely to change, especially in meeting challenges posed by new technologies and a global society, and how continuing education should update public relations professionals about their ethical responsibilities. One of the great pleasures and challenges of working in public relations is the knowledge that the profession is evolving—that standards of professionalism will continue to be shaped by current and future practitioners.

To provide further context for all these matters, the book presents in an appendix the Public Relations Society of America's Code of Professional Standards for the Practice of Public Relations and other code material.

This prefatory discussion of such a wide range of issues illustrates the intrinsic complexity of public relations ethics. Plenty of questions arise and generate still more questions. But answers can be found—ethical dilemmas can be resolved—as long as the commitment to high professional standards remains intact. That is what this book is about: pointing the way to ethical practices that match the principles, skills, and ambitions of the most conscientious public relations practitioners.

ACKNOWLEDGMENTS

We would like to thank our colleagues at Southern Methodist University for their interest in our work, and our colleagues around the country who share our belief in the importance of teaching ethics.

We particularly appreciate the efforts of Todd Hunt, Rutgers University; Dean Kruckeberg, University of Northern Iowa; Donald Wright, University of South Alabama; Deni Elliott, University of Montana; Maureen Rubin, California State University, Northridge; and Judy VanSlyke Turk, University of South Carolina, who reviewed our manuscript and offered many helpful suggestions.

Contents

PUBLIC RELATIONS ETHICS

CHAPTER ONE

The Public Relations Professional

Every profession has a moral purpose. Medicine has health. Law has justice. Public relations has harmony—social harmony.[1]

Through their work, public relations professionals promote mutual understanding and peaceful coexistence among individuals and institutions. They serve as a vital link in the communications process, making the remote proximate and demystifying the arcane. Whether representing a corporation, a presidential candidate, a charitable organization, or any other entity, public relations professionals keep information flowing among their employers and clients and their constituents.

At the highest level, public relations professionals counsel client organizations regarding the public implications of decisions and ensure that organizational actions are in the best interest of not only the organization, but also of those affected by the actions. This is not always an easy task, as pointed out by industry pioneer Ivy Lee as long ago as 1926.

"When I started in this work, it seemed to me there were two courses open to me. I could tell my clients what they wanted me to tell them. That, of course, would please them. But it would never get me very far. The other course was to tell them what I thought, irrespective of their opinions. If I were wrong I would soon find it out. In either case I'd eventually find my level."[2]

Lee's words came at a time when American business was viewed with suspicion and contempt by much of the public, a time when many companies operated under a "the public be damned" philosophy based on keeping organizational information under close wraps. Lee and other early public relations practitioners were instrumental in convincing institutions that the public could no longer be ignored if American institutions were to succeed. In order to survive in the new "consumer" society, organizations would have to respond to public concerns with more than merely lip service and would have to open up channels of communication.

According to Professor Mark McElreath, "Lee embraced the idea that an informed public was society's best safeguard against social ills. He aggressively demonstrated to the managers of a variety of organizations how they could win public support over time by consistently providing the publics with accurate information. He had a great deal of faith in the value of an informed individual in a free society."[3]

The efforts of Lee and other industry pioneers laid the groundwork for development of the management function that has come to be referred to by some as the "social conscience" of organizations. That function, of course, is public relations, and its members are charged with helping client organizations maintain positive relationships with the groups or individuals who influence the organizations' ability to operate successfully. Today's practitioners ideally serve as senior advisors to top management in positions that allow them to participate in the decision-making process. Operating on the premise that a company must deserve a favorable reputation if it is to maintain one, public relations professionals advise client companies to adapt to changing conditions and societal expectations, rather than to try to manipulate the environment for the good of the organization. Serving the public interest while serving one's own has always been the hallmark of good public relations work.

Unfortunately, today's practitioners find themselves operating in an environment in which efforts to "reform" socially irresponsible companies seem to have been only marginally successful. Almost three-quarters of a century after Lee and his counterparts succeeded in opening the eyes of American institutions to the power of public opinion, American society faces another crisis involving a lack of public trust.

THE ETHICS CRISIS: PERCEPTIONS AND REALITY

Today's crisis is not caused by a lack of communication. Rather, it is based on Americans' lack of confidence in their society's institutions. Questions of responsibility and ethics have become the cause of much concern and discourse in all segments of society.[4] The "ethics crisis" is a familiar topic in corporate boardrooms, university classrooms, and many other forums.[5]

Daily news coverage of executive missteps, illegal activity, and socially irresponsible behavior on the part of a variety of organizations has become commonplace. Many believe that the situation will get worse before it gets better. Michael Josephson, ethics consultant to some of America's largest companies, predicts that a "phenomenal number" of business scandals will surface during the 1990s. "We are swimming in enough lies to keep the lawyers busy for the next ten years," he says.[6]

The Institute for Crisis Management reports that news coverage of business crises increased 45 percent from 1991 to 1992 alone, with increasing focus on management decisions and their impact on business.[7] The institute predicts that the most newsworthy crisis categories in the coming years will be class-action lawsuits, business crimes, executive dismissals, judicial actions, and consumerism actions.[8]

Constant scrutiny of American institutions by the media and general public has not been lost on business leaders, as a recent study by Opinion Research Corporation shows. A survey of corporate executives found that 36 percent rated corporate America "fair" to "poor" in maintaining credibility with the public.[9] One wonders why anyone is surprised that the public lacks trust in these same institutions.

While the organizations they work for are being criticized for unethical practices, so are the professionals who participate in the decision-making processes of these organizations. The ethical sensitivity of all professionals has come into question in recent years.[10]

Because of their roles as both counselors and messengers, public relations professionals are targeted perhaps more than any others for allegedly unethical conduct. In the minds of some, organizations' success in eliminating questionable business practices is directly related to the ability of public relations professionals to assist organizations in becoming more socially responsible.

Public relations industry leader John Budd has observed that, to him, "the real issue of ethics is not so much how well we know the rules and stipulations but how we counsel on the subject. If we really do an effective job the true ethical violations will be more the exception than yet another example of the moral decay believed by some to be endemic in business."[11]

Michael Winkelman, former editor of the *Public Relations Journal*, echoes these thoughts. "For public relations professionals, the ethics crisis plays two ways: in terms of the ethics of the profession itself, and in terms of how maintaining ethical practices reflects on the reputations of the organizations for which public relations professionals work."[12]

In addition to working for "bad" companies, there are other reasons why public relations is getting a bad rap. Opinions about public relations are often affected by lack of clarity about just who the true public relations professionals are. Even journalists, who have frequent, direct contact with public relations practitioners, sometimes are uninformed or misinformed about the true nature of public relations work. One practitioner suggests that "perceptions of our discipline have been distorted over time by a parade of hacks, flacks and assorted charlatans who have adopted 'public relations' as a prestigious synonym of press agentry or publicity."[13]

Others believe that the image of public relations is undermined in more subtle ways. For example, researchers have found what they have termed "an insidious bias toward public relations" in introductory textbooks used in college mass communication courses. General disparagement in these texts is not offset by the authors' condescending recognition of professional codes of conduct and honest practitioners.[14] Such material implies that public relations professionals work under the burden of a presumption of guilt—that they are unethical until proved otherwise.

Study after study points out the need for improvement in ethical practices in public relations.[15] In one poll that addressed the state of public relations in 1992, business executives cited ethical lapses as the most negative development for the profession that year, and they declared ethics to be the greatest challenge facing the field today.[16]

The International Public Relations Association has regularly discussed the poor worldwide reputation of the profession and the lack of public understanding of the benefits that practitioners provide.[17]

Some of these concerns have nebulous bases, but others are rooted in hard fact. Two examples that resulted in embarrassing headlines for the public relations industry: Anthony Franco resigned his presidency of (and his membership in) the Public Relations Society of America in 1986 after signing a Securities and Exchange Commission (SEC) consent decree related to charges of insider trading; Michael Deaver, public relations professional and top aide in the Reagan White House, was convicted of perjury in 1987 after being investigated for violations of ethics laws.[18]

So, while the media and others have fanned the flame of misperception to some extent, bad acts on the part of practitioners certainly have added to the problem. When unethical individual actions are combined with the prevailing misperceptions about what public relations people do and the common view that public relations professionals who represent unethical companies are themselves unethical, it is no wonder that the morality of practitioners is being questioned.

This situation has created defensiveness on the part of some practitioners and a sense of futility on the part of others. Consider Daniel Edelman's assessment of the profession's ethical status: "We've seen a series of developments that have cast a black cloud over the public relations field. It's been bad enough that we've had to fight against the recession. That's been compounded by the questions that have been raised so widely through the media regarding our ethics, and our sense of morality, decency, accuracy, fairness and professionalism. I feel it's urgent that we recommit ourselves to honesty, integrity and full disclosure. We've got to maintain our high standards in judging who we're going to represent and what we're going to do for them . . ."[19]

Although Edelman believes that the profession's ethical standing can be improved, some of his colleagues appear to have given up the fight. According to E.W. Brody, "More and more practitioners . . . no longer identify themselves as public relations practitioners. The term 'public relations' appears nowhere on their firms' letterheads or business cards or in their literature. Words such as 'public communication' and 'public affairs' are used with increasing frequency."[20]

Such retreating is unfortunate because it could be perceived as an admission that the public relations profession is not honorable. Also, it provides absolutely no constructive help toward remedying the ethical shortcomings that do exist. However harshly one may judge the ethics of some members of a profession, clearly the field as a whole is not beyond redemption; it does not deserve the sweeping condemnation implicit in the abandonment of "public relations" as the description of this work.

In fact, in 1987 after a lengthy study, a PRSA Special Committee on Terminology led by Philip Lesly set forth recommendations that called for the use of the term *public relations* rather than alternatives. After noting that "the babel of terms applied to what is generally referred to as 'public relations' is a threat to the advancement of the field and to the stature of the people in it," the committee recommended that *public relations* was the only term that could provide a suitable "umbrella" characterization of the variety of functions encompassed in the practice.[21] The committee further recommended that practitioners be persuaded to use the proper term for a given function: "'Publicity' or 'promotion,' for example, should not be used as a synonym for public relations, but as only a specialized phase of it."[22]

Some members of the profession are moving aggressively in this direction. Rather than back down when attacked, they respond assertively. As one professional puts it: "Individual practitioners should also challenge unjust general criticism of public relations—no critical article in a newspaper should go unchallenged. No offhand, patronizing, critical or dismissive comment by business or social acquaintance should be allowed to stand without response. We should avoid . . . condoning the criticism of some mythical 'unethical' practitioner when the critic says, 'We realize it is not you but it is other people.'"[23]

While some argue that state licensing is the only way to rid the field of unscrupulous practitioners and to gain widespread credibility, most agree that ultimately it will not be the states, but rather the individuals who make up the industry, who will determine the future of this field.

The cumulative behavior of individual practitioners will determine the ethical standards and the perceived commitment to ethics of the profession. As Professors Todd Hunt and James Grunig observe, "It is very important to remember that small ethical lapses collectively chip away at the larger credibility of the public relations profession. Thus it is important for each practitioner to question every relationship and public communication in terms of its effect on the long-term viability of the profession."[24]

It is equally important for the practitioner to consider the social and professional responsibilities that accompany the role of a public relations counselor.

SOCIAL RESPONSIBILITIES

Because much of the distrust of public relations professionals derives from the lack of public trust in the institutions they represent, public relations professionals face a threefold task in improving their reputation. They must improve their position both with the public and the organizations they represent and also improve the social responsibility of client organizations.[25]

The concept of social responsibility recognizes the linkages between organizations and society and imposes an obligation on organizational leaders to consider the impact of decisions on those affected by them. As Professor S. Andrew Ostapski points out, "a corporation cannot fulfill its moral obligations by merely engaging in external acts of philanthropy. Instead, it must identify any harm it could inflict on society and respond to that harm."[26]

The good news is that the increasing focus on social good in organizational decision making creates an opportunity for public relations professionals to assume increased authority and higher-ranking positions within the organizational hierarchy. As public relations professionals claim more seats at board tables, both their ability to influence socially responsible behavior and their credibility with their organizations and the public will be improved.

In reality, public relations professionals' participation in organizational decision making varies considerably from institution to institution. Some practitioners are routinely involved in important policy decisions, while others are relegated to low-level technical functions.

Those who still find themselves implementing someone else's policies might think about why they remain in technical positions and consider broadening their level of expertise and skills. Until public relations practitioners have the ability to take a broad view of the organizations for which they work, they will likely not be invited to participate in decision making.[27]

If public relations professionals don't seek out and perform well in policy-making roles, they risk additional harm to both their credibility and their positions as senior advisors. It has been suggested, for example, that lawyers may be better suited to serve as ethics advisors for corporations. A past president of the American Bar Association proposed that "corporate legal counsel is uniquely situated and prepared to act as an arbiter to social conflict between the corporation and society and also to lend 'a deep sense of personal morality' to this task."[28]

It is arguable that such reasoning more aptly applies to public relations professionals than to lawyers. John D. Francis, a past president of the Canadian Public Relations Society, writes:

> Professional public relations practitioners are uniquely suited to fill the apparent void in ethics and social responsibility that exists in many organizations today, and to take the "long view." Assuming this role at the highest management level has a direct impact on the bottom line—in the long-term business considerations, public trust in government institutions, and public support of nonprofit organizations. It is a role we must accept, both in the theoretical terms of ethics and support of the public good, and in the pragmatic terms of being the essential and expedient instrument of an organization's formulation of successful policy. We must seize the challenge and make ourselves heard in the boardrooms of the nation.[29]

Francis offers the Exxon Valdez oil spill as an example of this void that public relations practitioners could fill: "This is a case of a company's listening to its brokers and lawyers instead of its public relations advisors and the public. Exxon's responses have been laced with references to the minimal impact on the bottom line to reassure the financial markets, and with efforts to minimize the company's legal liability. Neither of these strategies has succeeded. The company has been forced to spend more and more money and has been sued from all directions. The loss of public trust and goodwill is permanent. This is a traumatic experience for a previously well-respected company."[30]

Constructive intervention by public relations professionals might have helped minimize damage to Exxon's reputation. Instead, by not giving public relations its proper role in the information chain, the company left itself much more vulnerable than it needed to be to attacks from the public, press, and government.

Incidents as dramatic and headline-grabbing as the Exxon Valdez are not commonplace, although more and more companies are finding themselves the targets of negative publicity concerning bad acts. The value of solid public relations counsel both prior to and during such occurrences cannot be overstated. Honest, thoughtful, forthright communicating is the essence of public relations and should be an integral part of the information flow. (For more discussion on the Exxon Valdez case and other crises, see Chapter Eight.)

Of course, as Francis points out, the lawyers, as well as the financial and other advisors, have roles to play in devising socially responsible business practices. "But the table is set for one more in the '90s. The public relations professional is trained to look at both management's point of view and the public's. The public relations professional knows how to find out what the public is thinking, relay that to management, and formulate communications programs to increase public understanding and alter public attitudes toward the organization."[31]

POWER AND INFLUENCE AND PROFESSIONAL RESPONSIBILITY

For many public relations professionals, the silver lining in the cloud of public outcry about the ethics of public relations is the fact that at long last public relations is being recognized as both a legitimate management function and as one that wields enough power and influence to warrant public scrutiny.

Others, however, would just as soon continue to operate in virtual obscurity. In his book *Power Public Relations*, Leonard Saffir says that "savvy public relations professionals tend to play down the giant strength of the [public relations] discipline rather than draw attention to it."[32] One reason for soft-pedaling the real power of public relations, he says, is fear of backlash, or public criticism of techniques used to sway public opinion. Critics don't complain that public relations works badly, Saffir points out, but rather that it works only too well.[33]

Those critics are right. And the scrutiny is justified. The effects of public relations decisions are far-reaching and touch many lives.

Such impact demands that practitioners carefully examine the consequences of their decisions and programs. Whether trying to get a political candidate elected, regain a corporation's credibility following a crisis, or inform the nation about a new treatment for cancer, the means for doing so and the end result must be considered. Concern for the common good must be carefully weighed against organizational objectives.

Growth in professional power is accompanied by ethical responsibilities.[34] As professionals, public relations practitioners are held
accountable for their actions. The more influential any individual or
profession is, the greater the need for ethics. As public relations techniques become more sophisticated and as the field becomes further
integrated into the operations of business, government, and other
entities seeking representation, ethical perspectives must broaden
accordingly.

In a study of the relationship between professionals and society,
James Gaa points out that the autonomy provided to professionals
implies a concomitant obligation to society to regulate the profession
in such a way that the benefits to society are maximized. "Socially
responsible behavior is the quid pro quo, the price professionals must
pay to society for their autonomy."[35]

John Carey, author of *Professional Ethics of Certified Public
Accountants*, observes, "By definition, a professional service requires,
among other things, advanced intellectual training, mastery of technical subject matter, the exercise of skilled and responsible judgment.
These attributes are beyond appraisal by the client . . . the client must
take the professional man on faith—faith in his competence and faith
in his motives."[36]

Carey writes that the basic reason professionals are distinguished
from businesses and enjoy the prestige that accompanie professional
status is that "they are presumed to accept a special obligation to place
service ahead of personal gain."[37] The PRSA Counselors Academy's
Interpretations to the PRSA Code of Professional Standards states that
counselors have "an overriding responsibility to carefully balance
public interests with those of their clients, and to place both those
interests above their own."

As advocates for their client organizations, public relations practitioners face the special ethical demand that their advocacy not
become zealotry in the sense that the pursuit of "winning" becomes
all-consuming, sweeping before it any behavioral standards that might
obstruct the path to victory for the client or cause. This is not to say
that aggressive representation is improper, but that no matter how
noble the cause, the work should be done within ethical boundaries.

This is much the same responsibility that lawyers have when representing their clients. As advocates, attorneys must place their clients'
interests first, but not to the exclusion of all else. The temptation to do

that is very real; if yielded to, however, it can produce manipulated evidence, perjured testimony, and other tactics that may serve a client's short-term interest but that will also do long-term harm to the profession and to the entire justice system.

Professionals are bound to uphold industry standards as defined by the organizations that exist to serve the profession's members. Codes of professional conduct for public relations professionals have been around for almost fifty years. The Public Relations Society of America adopted its first statement of principles in 1950 and a code of professional standards in 1959. (See Exhibit 1.) Other communications organizations, both national and international, have guidelines similar to the PRSA Code.

PROFESSIONAL STANDARDS
for the
PRACTICE OF PUBLIC RELATIONS

AS MEMBERS of the PUBLIC RELATIONS SOCIETY OF AMERICA, we subscribe to the belief that inherent in the practice of public relations is the obligation of a public trust which requires fulfillment of these principles:

1. Objectives which are in full accord with the public welfare as well as the interests of our clients or employers.
2. Accuracy, truthfulness and good taste in material prepared for public dissemination and in all other activities sponsored, participated in or promoted, whether as independent public relations counsel or as officer or employee of a trade association, company or other organization or group;
3. Standards of practice which preclude the serving of competitors concurrently except with the full consent of all concerned; which safeguard the confidential affairs of client or employer even after termination of professional association with him and so long as his interests demand; and which, with full regard for our right to profit and to advance our personal interests, nevertheless preserve professional integrity as the primary concern of our work;

Exhibit continued

4. Cooperation with fellow practitioners in curbing malpractice such as the circulation of slanderous statements or rumors, the concealment from clients or employers of discounts or commissions, or any other information for professional gain or competitive advantage;
5. Support of efforts designed to further the ethics and technical proficiency of the profession and encourage the establishment of adequate training and education for the practice of public relations.

We realize full well that interpretation of a Code of Ethics becomes a matter of personal judgment in many instances, but we hold that a sincere effort to implement the spirit of the above principles will assure professional conduct of credit to the profession and honest service to clients and employers.

PUBLIC RELATIONS SOCIETY OF AMERICA
Adopted by the membership December 4, 1950

Reprinted with permission of the Public Relations Society of America

The PRSA Code has been updated several times, most recently in 1988, and its provisions have been amplified by formal PRSA interpretations. (See Chapter Two and the Appendix.)

Curbing the inclination to take advocacy too far requires more than adherence to professional codes of conduct, however. In the words of public relations scholar Raymond Simon, "It seems wise to be clear in our own minds about the point beyond which we are unwilling or unable to go and where we will not compromise." He also urges: "Keep constantly in mind that credibility underscores all effective communication. It is difficult to attain, more difficult to sustain, and once lost hard to regain."[38]

For public relations, as for other fields, professionalism is not created by decree. It must be earned, and its existence depends in great part on the eye of the beholder. Those who see public relations as merely a manipulative scam are unlikely to change their minds until a commitment to ethics becomes a more visible characteristic of public relations practices. And, from the standpoint of the practitioner, attainment of true professionalism occurs when thoughtful appreciation of ethics becomes a pervasive characteristic of those who work in this field.

As Butler University Professor Gay Wakefield puts it: "Societal demands placed upon business and government today have spurred a new level of accountability to which public relations professionals must be prepared to respond, both privately and publicly. Practitioners, educators and students need to accept ethical challenges as opportunities to channel private ethical beliefs into public actions demonstrating those commitments."[39]

The link between individual ethical behavior and the professionalism of the field is clearly unbreakable. Professional ethics derive from personal values. When confronting the question of how to improve their profession's credibility, public relations practitioners might consider the extent to which they themselves are responsible for their current image problems. The future of public relations will be determined by their individual and collective responses.

CHAPTER TWO

Ethical Decision Making in Public Relations

Almost every day public relations professionals face situations that test their moral resolve and force them to make hard choices. Often, there is no right or wrong answer to an ethical problem, simply alternate routes from which to choose. Consider the following hypotheticals:

You have been invited by a member of a graphic design firm to attend the opening night performance of a highly acclaimed new Broadway show. You know that the design firm is interested in securing a contract to produce your annual report. Do you accept?

In pitching a story to an industry publication, the editor indicates that she is interested in doing a feature on your company. She also suggests that the issue in which the story would run would provide a great opportunity for your organization to reach potential customers through advertising. How do you respond?

Your firm is going up against one of your fiercest competitors for a big corporate account that would secure your agency's place as a leader in the industry. You are asked by the potential client to comment on the abilities of the competing firm, which, in your opinion, always overstates its abilities. What do you say?

You have been asked to prepare a news release to address concerns about your company's involvement in illegal activities. Legal counsel tells you to simply deny any involvement on the part of your company. You have information that indicates that some illegal acts may have occurred. What do you do?

Your company has just entered a new foreign market and needs media coverage to establish your company's presence. You know that you can secure positive stories in a local publication by simply paying for them—a common practice in that area. What do you do?

A new client has asked you to plan an elaborate news conference to announce his candidacy for a judicial position in your city. You know that the media will likely not show up because he is relatively unknown in political circles. You also know he won't be satisfied with a news release. What do you recommend?

As the director of public relations for a national nonprofit organization, you are in charge of reporting your organization's annual revenue. The financial report you have received from your boss appears to overvalue the worth of donated goods. Although you appreciate the importance of providing prospective donors with evidence of past successes, you question the accuracy of the report. What do you do?

Your company has been experiencing the painful process of downsizing. Employee morale is down, and management is concerned that some of the best employees may leave to join more financially secure competitors. You are asked to prepare an employee announcement to inform employees that the layoffs are complete. You know that this is not true. What do you do?

Your agency has just been approached by a well-financed organization whose members oppose abortion. They seek your help with a national campaign to promote prolife philosophies. Although you and some of your staff don't support these views, you know it would be a lucrative account. What do you do?

Public relations professionals who face such dilemmas must identify potentially conflicting loyalties and clarify which should take precedence in particular situations. Five categories of duties can be identified: (1) duty to self, (2) duty to client organization, (3) duty to employer, (4) duty to profession, and (5) duty to society. In considering these duties, think about how loyalties should be prioritized in the preceding hypotheticals.

DUTY TO SELF

Professionals in public relations must first consider loyalty to self. They must define their own value system and decide which, if any, of those values they are willing to compromise in carrying out their professional obligations. A tough question is whether personal values should ever be sacrificed for the sake of the firm or client.

DUTY TO CLIENT ORGANIZATION

Many professional services providers believe that the professional's first loyalty should be to the client organization that he or she agrees to represent. Determining just how far that loyalty should go presents a particularly troublesome issue for public relations professionals. First, as public relations advocates, do you represent the client organization itself or merely the client's "cause"? Second, does an agreement to serve as a client's agent create a fiduciary relationship that requires special duties on the part of the public relations professional to safeguard the client's interests?

DUTY TO EMPLOYER

Where does loyalty to the one who signs the paycheck end? Determining when organizational loyalty may be misplaced involves agonizing decisions on the part of employees. Professional disagreements about the way a company operates is one thing; condoning activities that place others at risk of harm is another. The professional who knowingly allows potentially harmful deeds to continue violates his duty to the public, which must take precedence over duty to the employing organization.

DUTY TO PROFESSION

A public relations professional has an obligation to support his or her chosen profession and the colleagues with whom he or she associates. Some suggest that if public relations is to be considered a professional discipline rather than a technical skill, then practitioners must be responsible to their peers. According to one scholar, "The true professional will place recognition from fellow public relations [practitioners] above recognition from an employer, while a careerist will indicate more concern for acceptance from an organizational superior who has input into salaries and promotions."[1] Does this mean that a corporate counselor who is asked to perform in a way that violates the PRSA Code of Ethics should risk losing his or her position with the company to uphold industry principles?

DUTY TO SOCIETY

Service to society is a key component of every profession and high on the list of professional values. The PRSA Code of Professional Standards, for example, states in article 1, "A member shall conduct his or her professional life in accord with the public interest." As in many other fields, however, specific guidelines for how to do so are lacking. How is "public interest" defined and what is required of public relations professionals to serve that interest?

The nature of the public relations function and the variety of ways in which it is practiced create special difficulties in clarifying how public interest can best be served. The four public relations practice models proposed by Professors James Grunig and Todd Hunt illustrate this point.

Under the press agentry, or publicity, model, the purpose of communication is merely to get information placed in the mass media to gain recognition. Common examples of press agentry are found in the attempts of politicians and celebrities to increase name recognition. The public information model is also a one-sided approach to communication in which the practitioner serves the journalistic function of making objective-but-favorable information about the company available to the company's publics. In applying the more sophisticated two-way asymmetric approach, professionals conduct social science research to gather information that helps in adjusting messages to influence the behavior of publics.

In contrast to these unilateral approaches, practitioners take on the role of mediators in the two-way symmetric model and promote understanding between an organization and its constituents. This model incorporates the idea that both the organization and its publics may change in maintaining positive relationships.[2]

According to Professor Grunig, the two-way symmetrical approach may be the only ethical way to practice public relations. "[I]n spite of the good intentions of practitioners—it is difficult, if not impossible, to practice public relations in a way that is ethically and socially responsible using an asymmetric model" that attempts to change the behavior of publics without changing the behavior of the organization.[3]

Grunig explains that the two-way symmetrical approach avoids the problem of ethical relativism because it defines ethics as a process of public relations rather than as an outcome. "Symmetrical public relations provides a forum for dialogue, discussion, and discourse on issues for which people with different values generally come to different conclusions. As long as the dialogue is structured according to ethical rules, the outcome should be ethical—although not usually one that fits the value system of any competing party perfectly."[4]

Public relations scholar Thomas Bivins questions whether any of the four models can be reconciled with a duty to serve the public interest. "How can a practitioner advocating a discrete point of view serve the interest of the greater public? Does a practitioner acting as a mediator serve only the two parties involved in the issue at hand, or is the greater public benefited in some way?"[5]

In a study of these issues, Bivins suggests four possible paradigms for serving the public interest:

First, if every individual practicing public relations acts in the best interest of his or her client, then the public interest will be served.

Second, if, in addition to serving individual interests, an individual practicing public relations serves public interest causes, the public interest will be served.

Third, if a profession or professionals assure that every individual in need of or desiring its/their services receives its/their services, then the public interest will be served.

Fourth, if public relations as a profession improves the quality of debate over issues important to the public, then the public interest will be served.[6]

None of these approaches provides the definitive answer. Such analysis does, however, demonstrate the need for individual practitioners to consider how they can best fulfill their obligation to society. According to Bivins:

> It is left to the individual practitioners to discharge what they believe to be a tacit obligation to society through either the competent carrying out of their normal functions which will somehow ultimately contribute to the well-being of society as a whole,

or by such means as pro bono work which, although admirable, is still service to a special interest. Neither is it practical nor necessary to attempt to provide for equal service to all who need it as do the legal and medical professions. Equal availability (emphasized), while sufficient, is also not enough to satisfy the obligation to contribute to the public interest.[7]

Bivins concludes his study by suggesting that the true answer to what constitutes public service might be found in examining what public relations is designed to do. "In its dual role as mediator and advocate, public relations has the opportunity both to engage in and to encourage public debate. By doing so, it also has the opportunity, and the obligation, to lessen the obfuscation often surrounding the mere provision of information. It must develop clear guidelines and formal mechanisms by which the issues important to society are clarified and presented to the public for open, democratic debate."[8]

A related question involving the prioritization of these diverse duties is who should be held accountable for making these decisions—the individual practitioner, the industry, or the client organizations for whom practitioners work?

ACCOUNTABILITY

In business settings, numerous individuals may be involved in the ethical decision-making process. Both staff members and outside counselors may be consulted regarding a client organization's policies and actions. Although the ultimate decision rests with the organization's executives, each individual's role in the process should not be ignored. The fact that one gives ethical advice that is not followed doesn't necessarily get that person off the hook when a company makes a bad decision.

Although an organization may be viewed as having a "life" of its own, organizational decisions result from individual moral reasoning. The individuals who represent the organizational entity will ultimately be held accountable for the actions of the institution. Those involved in the process will be judged according to the measure of their responsibility and involvement.[9]

In *Media Ethics*, the authors state that "responsibility, to be meaningfully assigned and focused, must be distributed among the individuals constituting the corporations. Individuals are not wholly discrete, unrelated, atomistic entities; they always stand in a social context with which they are morally involved. But individuals they nevertheless remain. And it is with each person that ethics is fundamentally concerned."[10]

Marketing Professor Gene Laczniak points out that although a variety of factors influence the decision-making process, individual values are the final standard, although not necessarily the determining reason for ethical behavior. "[N]o matter what factors lead a manager to make a particular decision there is a measure of individual responsibility that cannot be denied because in the last analysis the decision was made by a given manager."[11]

Thus, the moral character of the decision makers is a primary factor in determining whether an organization acts ethically. The values of the individuals who influence the decision-making process will essentially determine the values of the organization and, therefore, the principles upon which decisions will be based. As ethics advisors, public relations professionals can play critical roles in helping organizations institutionalize ethical values.

DEFINING VALUES

Defining the ethical values that should guide behavior begins with the recognition that ethics is not simply a matter of opinion. Michael Josephson, founder of the Josephson Institute for the Advancement of Ethics, states that "[i]t is critical to effective ethics education to overcome the cynicism of ethical relativism—the view that ethics is just a matter of opinion and personal belief as in politics and religion. Though debatable beliefs regarding sexual matters and religion often do travel under the passport of morality, there are ethical norms that transcend cultures and time."[12]

Josephson has identified ten universal and timeless values that, he says, are essential to the ethical life. Those values are: (1) honesty, (2) integrity, (3) promise-keeping, (4) fidelity, (5) fairness, (6) caring for others, (7) respect for others, (8) responsible citizenship, (9) pursuit of excellence, and (10) accountability.[13] According to Josephson, these core values provide the foundation for isolating ethical issues and beginning the decision-making process.

Although it is difficult to prioritize these values, one might simplify the process by emphasizing a commitment to integrity, which encompasses other important values. *Integrity* is defined as being of "sound moral principle."[14] The term incorporates the concepts of honesty and fairness, which have been identified as two of the most important factors in ethical decision making.

Following an intense literature search for ethical absolutes that educators might teach students, Professor Mel Sharpe found two concepts that qualified: honesty and fairness. Sharpe concluded that these two ethical absolutes "can be defined also as the behavior required to create and maintain harmony in human relationships."[15]

Honesty, of course, means free from deceit or fraud. *Fair* is defined as just and impartial. *Just* refers to one who is upright and honorable. *Upright* implies an unbending moral straightness, that is, integrity.

So that's where defining values begins and ends—with good, old-fashioned integrity. This universally accepted standard is one to which ethical individuals and organizations subscribe.

Much like the "lessons" in Robert Fulghum's popular little book *All I Really Need to Know I Learned in Kindergarten*, the wisdom of such thought lies in its simplicity. The challenge for professionals lies in translating these seemingly simple values into ethical principles that guide behavior and create social harmony. As Fulghum says, knowing what is right is one thing. "Living it—well that's another matter, yes?"[16]

ESTABLISHING ETHICAL PRINCIPLES

Ethical principles derive from ethical values and form the "rules" by which ethical behavior is judged. In resolving ethical dilemmas, professionals often look first to the law for such guidance. Because legal behavior generally includes ethical behavior, the law is sometimes viewed as having a "halo" of morality.[17] As a basis for moral responsibilities, however, the law is limited in value. Although the law articulates what is believed to be morally right today, it stops short of providing a blueprint for ethical behavior. As the U.S. Supreme Court said in *Miami Herald* v. *Tornillo*, virtue cannot be legislated.

Where the law ends is often where ethics begins. Ethical issues sometimes arise when the law or legal precedents are either unclear or at variance with shifting cultural values or are perceived as not going far enough to protect public welfare.[18]

Business crises provide excellent examples of organizations being publicly condemned for acts that are perfectly legal. Environmental activities, in particular, have come under fire in recent years. Although a company may be in compliance with legal air-quality standards, it may still be perceived as not acting in a socially acceptable manner.

Ethics requires more than mere technical compliance with the law. Ethical individuals and organizations "consciously advance ethical principles by choosing to do more than they have to and less than they have a [legal] right to do."[19]

In the absence of laws, professionals might consult industry and company codes of conduct for direction in defining acceptable behavior. Such codes are designed to translate the more formal philosophical theories of ethics into a set of guidelines that can be applied to routine decision making.

In public relations, for example, several codes of conduct exist. The PRSA Code of Professional Standards applies to the more than seventeen thousand members of PRSA. In addition, the International Association of Business Communicators, the International Public Relations Association, and other such organizations also offer codes for their members. (See Appendix.)

The advantage of such codes is found in the number of professionals who are a part of designing and then implementing the standards. The disadvantage is that in achieving this breadth, specificity is often sacrificed. The final product might be a high-minded articulation of general philosophy, but it may be so vague that it provides little help to the practitioner grappling with difficult on-the-job ethical problems.

Critics of the PRSA Code have noted both a "glittering lack of precision" within the code and a lack of consensus among practitioners about how code provisions should be interpreted. Researchers have found that professionals suggest different responses when queried about the same ethical issues, "suggesting the presence of subjectiveness as the prevailing moral-ethical theory in public relations."[20]

Additionally, enforcement of the code is limited by the sponsoring organization's authority. PRSA sanctions range from admonishment to expulsion from the organization. That is a far cry from the punitive power wielded by organizations in professions in which practitioners are licensed. For example, state bar associations can launch disbarment proceedings against lawyers who violate their canons of ethics. Such measures can result in the permanent barring of the wrongdoer from the profession.

Such complaints illustrate the difficulty in designing an effective code of ethics. Code drafters are challenged to devise comprehensive guidelines that incorporate professional values and clearly establish expectations of behavior.

The best codes explain the ethical philosophy behind ethical behavior such that practitioners are stimulated to think about not only what is right or wrong, but also why it is right or wrong. These codes also distinguish minimum standards of conduct from ideal goals by directing code provisions to the work of the average, conscientious professional—not solely to the behavior of an ethics superhero.

In order to be truly effective, codes of ethics must have teeth—they must be enforceable and enforced. Additionally, codes must be viewed as "living documents" designed to encourage ongoing review with an eye toward expansion and revision.[21] Only through proper enforcement and appropriate revision will a code of ethics successfully guide the work of professionals in an ever-changing world.

In an attempt to provide detailed ethical direction for public relations professionals, PRSA has issued "official interpretations" of several articles in its code, spelling out more specifically what is deemed ethical and what is not. Additionally, the PRSA Counselors Academy has developed special interpretations for members of counseling firms. (See Appendix.) Such specificity is both helpful and necessary if practitioners are truly to understand what actions might be categorized as unethical.

One significant problem with the PRSA Code has little to do with its content, and a lot to do with its impact. Although the code applies to more public relations professionals than does any other code in the communications field, it still is enforceable only as to PRSA members, who constitute only 10 percent or fewer of active public relations professionals.[22] This means that the vast majority of practitioners are not guided by formal industry standards of conduct. Obviously, considerable work is needed to change this situation if the ethical practice of public relations is to be improved.

Many public relations firms and departments have supplemented the existing industry codes with their own codes of conduct. In-house codes have become standard operating practice for some agency professionals, who make a habit of giving new clients copies of both the PRSA Code and their own code of ethics.

Additionally, public relations professionals are becoming more involved in the development of codes of conduct for the companies they represent. Recognizing the negative impact of being viewed as socially irresponsible, more and more companies are integrating ethics into their company culture and instituting clear, written guidelines for employee conduct. According to one report, more than 80 percent of the Fortune 500 companies have taken steps to institutionalize ethical standards in their decision-making processes.[23]

Although internal codes have been criticized as being "no more than promotional efforts, geared toward image-making and enforcement of employee loyalty," they can be helpful in improving ethical practices, according to W. Michael Hoffman of Bentley College's Center for Business Ethics. "Good will result regardless of the intentions. Corporations are making progress by seeking to institute ethics in corporate activities. It gives employees safety, something to go back to."[24] Of course, as Hoffman adds, the benefits of these codes are contingent on the company's willingness to enforce its own rules.[25]

Citicorp and Martin Marietta have been identified as two corporations that do enforce ethical rules. These companies have come up with creative strategies, including board games called The Work Ethic and Gray Matters, respectively, to help employees understand and implement the companies' ethical policies.[26] Corporate leaders say that such techniques help establish a dialogue on ethical issues and get employees to take ethics seriously. "You can't overstate the importance of talking about ethics," says Kate Nelson, Citicorp's head of communication for corporate human resources. "Without training, even well-meaning employees can make bad decisions."[27]

Communicating ethical principles also sends the message that unethical behavior will not be tolerated. Professor Ronald Sims points out that employees sometimes commit unethical actions because organizations reward behaviors that violate ethical standards.[28] Organizational "counternorms," he says, are responsible for managerial values that undermine integrity. For example, the bottom-line mentality often supports financial success as the only value to be considered.

Changing this kind of thinking, or establishing a more ethical operating climate, is the responsibility of top managers, Sims suggests. "What top managers do, and the culture they establish and reinforce, makes a big difference in the way lower-level employees act and in the way the organization as a whole acts when ethical dilemmas are faced."[29] Using the Johnson & Johnson Tylenol crisis as an example, Sims notes that company executives sent a signal to employees by immediately pulling their product from the marketplace. "[T]hey knew that 'the J & J way' was to do the right thing regardless of its cost. What they were implicitly saying was that the ethical framework of the company required that they act in good faith in this fashion."[30]

Organizational culture—the shared understanding of ethical values and of what constitutes ethical behavior—sets the tone for decision making at all levels in the organization. As both policymakers and technicians, public relations professionals play important roles in organizational efforts to establish positive cultures and institutionalize ethical practices. At Citicorp, for example, senior management turned to corporate communications to develop a program that would establish an ethical corporate culture and encourage compliance with ethical principles.[31]

Public relations industry leaders and scholars believe that public relations professionals will play increasingly important roles as ethics advisors. Professor Fraser Seitel notes that "[a]s the internal conscience of many organizations, the public relations department has become a focal point for the institutionalization of ethical conduct. Increasingly, management has turned to public relations officers to lead the internal ethical charge, to be the keeper of the organizational ethic."[32]

Public relations senior counselors particularly have an opportunity to influence ethical decision making. People in these positions should take a broad view of the potential impact of organizational decisions and ensure that the ethics of actions is considered along with legal and financial impact.

Practitioners who perform primarily technical duties can also influence ethical behavior by communicating to employees and other publics the organization's mission, vision, values, and ethics.[33] Such efforts help to establish an environment in which unethical actions are exceptions rather than the norm.

By helping to raise the ethical standard of the organizations they represent, public relations professionals will enhance their own reputation. By further cultivating their own ethical competence, practitioners will also define their future as organizational ethics advisors.

CHAPTER THREE

Understanding Ethics

Before plunging into the tumult of on-the-job ethical decision making, the public relations professional should think about ethics per se. The nature of public relations work demands quick reactions with little time for reflection. The process by which choices are made and decisions reached is important. Having an understanding of the philosophy of ethics may make the practice of ethics easier and improve the quality of the decisions reached.

As a discipline, ethics involves the study of standards of human conduct and moral judgment.[1] In a broad sense, ethics can be defined as the criteria by which decisions are made about what is right and what is wrong.[2] For individuals and organizations, ethics means defining individual and societal values that are morally acceptable and demonstrating a commitment to uphold those values. In other words, ethics means going beyond simply voicing an intention to do the right thing and actually incorporating ethics into everyday life.

Varied methods have been proposed for evaluating the ethics of particular actions. The two most common are broadly categorized as *teleological*, a results-oriented approach that defines ethical behavior on the basis of either good or bad consequences, and *deontological*, an act-oriented approach that emphasizes the intrinsic worth or value of the action itself. Understanding the theory behind these approaches helps both to stimulate the moral imagination and to assist in the development of analytical skills required for ethical decision making.

TELEOLOGICAL APPROACH

Teleology derives from two Greek words: *telo* and *logos*. *Teleo* refers to "end" and *logos* to "the study of." Thus, *teleology* means the "study of ends." This approach is applied by "utilitarian" philosophers who propose that the usefulness of acts, measured by how much pleasure will be produced, should be considered most important in determining ethical behavior. Utilitarians examine the utility of certain actions in improving human life and find that the ethical alternative is the one that produces the greatest balance of good over evil.

On the surface, the utilitarian approach, or simply looking at the consequences that result from a particular act, appears to be an easy way to evaluate ethical behavior. A problem exists, however, because one must act before knowing the outcome of his or her action. A means for measuring potential good must be devised.

Jeremy Bentham, a British philosopher and early leader in utilitarian thought, provided some guidance in this area. Using what he called the "hedonistic calculus," Bentham identified seven factors by which an act should be measured: (1) the intensity of the feeling, (2) its duration, (3) its certainty or uncertainty, (4) its propinquity or remoteness, (5) its fecundity (future), (6) its purity (the probability that pleasure or pain will result), and (7) its extent (or number of people affected). Bentham recommended that alternative actions should be evaluated according to these criteria by assigning scores for each factor, with the act producing the highest score, or most pleasure, considered most ethical.[3]

Some find such a utilitarian theory flawed for two primary reasons: (1) the focus is merely on the quantity of pleasure produced, rather than on the type, and (2) the theory could be used to justify even unethical behavior if the result is good. Questions raised focus on whether, in fact, all good is equal, and whether a good end can justify any means.

The approach also presents questions of conflict with regard to which segment of society should be considered most important. For example, as public relations scholar Mark McElreath points out, organizational decision-makers "might argue against making significant philanthropic contributions on the grounds that the money could be spent better producing an improved product which would yield a greater good not only for society but also for the organization."[4]

The issue of quality of pleasure was addressed by noted philosopher John Stuart Mill, who rejected the notion that all good is equal. Mill expanded utilitarian thinking by suggesting that both the quality of the good and the long-term (versus merely short-term) consequences of the act should be considered.[5]

In *Utilitarianism*, Mill writes:

> The creed which accepts as the foundation of moral "utility" or the "greatest happiness principle" holds that actions are right in proportion as they tend to promote happiness; wrong as they tend to produce the reverse of happiness. By happiness is intended pleasure and the absence of pain; by unhappiness, pain and the privation of pleasure . . . It is quite compatible with the principle of utility to recognize the fact that some kinds of pleasure are more desirable and more valuable than others. It would be absurd that, while in estimating all other things quality is considered as well as quantity, the estimation of pleasure should be supposed to depend on quantity alone.[6]

Of course, measuring quality of pleasure involves subjective analyses regarding what standards would be appropriate for making such determinations. Although Mill doesn't provide those standards, he does offer some examples of what he thinks should be considered "higher" or "lower" pleasures. Included among the higher pleasures are such things as intelligence, mental pleasure, and health. Among the lower are ignorance, stupidity, selfishness, indolence, and physical pleasures.[7] Later utilitarians expanded such thinking by arguing that values such as friendship, loyalty, and fairness also possess intrinsic worth.[8]

Ethics Professor Thomas White points out that although Bentham and Mill provide some valuable tools for ethical decision making, one's mind is the most important component in the teleological process. "[I]magination and judgment are important components in a results- or consequence-oriented approach to ethical analysis. . . . You need to use your imagination to figure out all of the possible consequences of an action. If you have a variety of options, you have to speculate about what pleasures and pains will follow from each action. And you certainly need your imagination to figure out the long-term consequences of the options."[9]

The practical value of utilitarian philosophy lies in the requirement that decision-makers conscientiously consider the consequences of particular actions. The benefits and risks of potential harm to everyone affected by a decision must be carefully weighed. The ethical course of action is that which maximizes benefits and minimizes harm.

DEONTOLOGICAL APPROACH

Contrary to teleologists, deontologists do not believe that the end can be used to justify the means. The term *deontology* derives from the Greek word *deontos*, which means "duty." Deontological theory is based on the premise that human beings are obligated to treat other human beings with dignity simply because they are human. Under this humanistic approach, people have a duty to respect other people's rights and to treat them accordingly.

Deontologists judge ethical behavior solely on the basis of whether the act itself is right or wrong. Rather than measuring pleasure and pain or good and bad, the deontological approach evaluates the extent to which actions conform to acceptable standards of human behavior. The Declaration of Independence is perhaps the best example of deontological thinking. This document guarantees human beings certain rights that cannot be violated by another. Actions that respect those rights are viewed as conforming to a basic concept of humanity.[10]

The Universal Declaration of Human Rights adopted by the United Nations in 1948 is another good example of humanistic thinking. This document describes the needs of "all people and all nations" and lists thirty "rights" that humans need in order to enjoy a good life. As the Preamble states, "[R]ecognition of the inherent dignity and of the equal and inalienable rights of all members of the human family is the foundation of freedom, justice and peace in the world." (See the Appendix for the full text of the document.)

The deontological approach measures whether actions are morally right or wrong by evaluating whether they conform to these basic human rights. Most ethical issues can be traced to the principles embodied in this document. Ethical concerns surface when human needs and rights are violated.

According to Professor McElreath, public relations practitioners particularly should be familiar with this document and the principles it embodies. "Public relations professionals who recognize these basic rights will work to ensure their organizations and clients are engaged in ethical communications."[11]

Immanuel Kant, considered among the most important deontological thinkers, offers a simple test for ethical actions: Does the act represent personal freedom, choice, and autonomy?[12] Kant offers a principle called the "categorical imperative," which requires that actions be judged by whether they conform to the "moral law." If an act could be translated into an acceptable "universal" law that would apply to everyone faced with the same situation, then it would be considered ethically acceptable.[13]

The difficulty of deontological analysis lies in defining Kant's "moral law." There exists considerable disagreement regarding the scope of human rights, which rights and values are most important, and what constitutes a violation of those rights. While many values are widely shared, debate ensues in discussions of which actions best serve the public interest and are, therefore, socially acceptable.

Additionally, history shows that as societies develop and change, so do values and moral reasoning. Consider, for example, the abolition of slavery following the Civil War or the sexual revolution of the sixties—two very different issues that illustrate how definitions of socially acceptable behavior change.

Legal reasoning, which embodies the idea that laws should be modified to reflect modern thought, provides some insight into deontology. Negligence law's "reasonable person" concept, for example, is analogous to the deontologist's view that ethical acts must conform to socially acceptable behavior. In negligence cases, if the court finds that a "reasonable person" would have acted as the defendant did in the same or similar circumstances, then most likely the defendant will be declared not guilty.

Applying this concept to ethical thinking, one would consider whether a reasonable person would find particular acts offensive, that is, unethical. Although subjective in nature, this approach helps get beyond the intangible nature of defining the scope of human rights and values.

The "reasonable person" approach is not without its problems, however. Such reasoning suggests that acts can be classified as either good or bad according to whether other "reasonable" people would act in the same way. If American society is basically "bad," as some think, then bad acts become socially acceptable.

Professor White says, "Somewhere over the last quarter century, America has lost its 'moral rudder.' We have gone from a nation committed to moral idealism to being reluctant spectators of one scandal after another. We have seen so much wrongdoing in government, business, education, and even religion, that unethical behavior has simply become 'business as usual' in some quarters of the society. And what's the most telling sign of how bad it's become? We aren't even shocked anymore."[14]

But just because "everybody's doing it" doesn't make it right. Inherent in all ethical theories is the concept of choice—that humans choose to act in certain ways. Rather than look at how people are, ethicists look at how people can (or should) be.

Any efforts to "teach" people the importance of ethical decision making must be directed toward helping them become more aware of the important role that personal choice plays in that process. Professor David L. Martinson suggests, "The efforts should not be directed so much toward providing specific answers, but rather focus on helping individuals realize that there are ethical problems . . . and there are better or worse ways of trying to deal with them."[15]

ETHICAL REASONING

Regardless of whether one acts out of a sense of duty or of morality, ethical actions are viewed as the result of intellectual reasoning. Because humans have the ability to reason and analyze the implications of their actions, they are held both legally and morally accountable for their decisions.

Some think that ethics is not something that can be learned or taught like English or history since basic moral education occurs as part of the experience of growing up. In fact, university professors have struggled to come up with an acceptable and effective way to teach people how to be ethical. Although the majority of the country's business schools reportedly teach ethics, many academics admit that they have not been successful in reconciling the theory of business ethics with the reality of doing business.[16]

Moral philosophy is sometimes seen as too "academic" and not practical enough to offer true guidance for the working professional. One commentator finds that "[ethical] theorizing is . . . utterly inaccessible to the people for whom business ethics is not merely a subject of study but is (or will be) a way of life."[17]

In spite of such problems, there is widespread agreement that better decisions result from the study of ethics. Ethics advisors point out that because the attitudes and beliefs that make up a person's operational value system continue to change throughout adult life, it is never too late to influence ethical behavior.[18] Additionally, research suggests that managers need and welcome assistance in identifying appropriate courses of action in difficult ethical situations.[19]

One popular ethical decision-making model was devised by Ralph Potter of the Harvard Divinity School. Dubbed "The Potter Box," this approach involves four steps: (1) defining the situation, (2) identifying values, (3) selecting principles, and (4) choosing loyalties to stakeholders.[20] Such a process forces one to prioritize both the values and the publics that are most important in a given situation. This model is particularly useful to the public relations professional charged with identifying, establishing, and maintaining relationships with numerous constituents.

THE POTTER BOX APPROACH TO ETHICAL DECISION MAKING

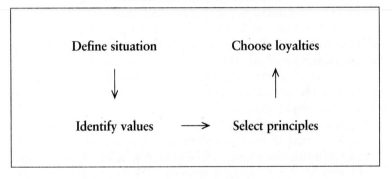

Consider the following example: You are the public relations director for Megabucks Energy Company, a Fortune 500 oil and gas exploration and production corporation. Megabucks has been experiencing the painful process of downsizing due to declining oil and gas prices. Drilling on one of the company's properties in the Java Sea has produced promising results of a significant new oil and gas well. Although testing has not been completed, rumors are flying in the marketplace about the potential of this new well to double Megabucks' profits. You recommend that a news release be issued to respond to these rumors, and senior executives ask you to prepare a release that downplays the significance of the find and states that additional drilling must be conducted before the size of the well can be defined. You have internal reports that indicate that company officials already know that this is a major discovery that will have a material impact on the company's profits. What do you do?

Applying the Potter Box approach, step 1 requires that the situation be analyzed and defined. You have been asked to disseminate deceptive information upon which a number of important publics will rely. When later reports show that, in fact, the well is a significant discovery, both you and your company may be perceived as unethical in dealing with its constituents. The possibility of legal sanctions is also very real.

Step 2 asks you to identify the values that are important in this situation. Honesty and fairness top the list here. What other values are important?

In step 3, ethical principles must be selected. The legality of reporting false data should first be considered—would the release violate SEC regulations? What about industry and company codes of conduct? How does the PRSA Code of Professional Standards deal with this issue? Would article 5 apply? What does your personal code of ethics require that you do?

Step 4 involves prioritizing stakeholders. Loyalties important in this situation would include (1) SEC, (2) shareholders, (3) employees, (4) financial media, (5) public, (6) company, (7) profession, and (8) self. How can these duties be reconciled in reaching a decision?

Another ethical decision-making model, suggested by Professor McElreath as an alternative to the Potter Box, is based on both the teleological and deontological theories.[21] This approach involves: (1) confrontation of an ethical dilemma, (2) individual motivation to act, (3) consideration of rules, principles, or duties based on authoritative sources, or predictions concerning causes and consequences of actions, or a combination of both, and (4) individual decision and action.

This method provides the option to consider either the consequences of the act or the act itself or both. Analyze the oil and gas company dilemma by applying this model. Would the same decision be reached?

Business Professor Ronald Sims offers the following practical approach for companies to use in helping employees resolve ethical dilemmas: (1) Recognize and clarify the dilemma, (2) get all the possible facts, (3) list your options—all of them, (4) test each option by asking, "Is it legal? Is it right? Is it beneficial?", (5) make your decision, (6) double-check your decision by asking: "How would I feel if my family found out about this? How would I feel if my decision was printed in the local newspaper?", and (7) take action.[22]

When faced with the challenge of coming up with an ethical decision-making model for a client's employees who were functionally illiterate, Frank Navran & Associates devised a six-step decision-making process that reflects what people do naturally when confronted with an ethical dilemma:

1. Define the problem.
2. Identify available alternative solutions.
3. Evaluate the identified alternatives.
4. Make the decision.
5. Implement the decision.
6. Evaluate the decision.

The ethical component of the process requires decision-makers to screen out ethical problems and solutions in steps 1, 3, and 6 by applying a set of "filters" referred to as "PLUS":

P = Policies		Is it consistent with my organization's policies, procedures, and guidelines?
L = Legal		Is it acceptable under applicable laws and regulations?
U = Universal		Does it conform to the universal principles/ values my organization has adopted?
S = Self		Does it satisfy my personal definition of right, good, and fair?

Navran notes that "users should realize that the PLUS filters do not guarantee an ethical decision. They merely ensure that the ethical components of the situation will be surfaced so that they might be considered . . . ultimately whether or not the decision meets the ethical standards of the organization or individual decision maker is a matter of personal responsibility. After all, ethics is about choices."[23]

In fact, none of these approaches is guaranteed to result in ethical decisions. Each requires subjective analysis, which introduces the element of moral character. Such models do, however, provide a framework for analyzing and understanding ethical problems.

Michael Josephson summarizes the need for such analysis. "In the 'real world' there are many shades of gray, even in routine decision making. Most of these decisions are made in the context of economic, professional, and social pressures which compete with ethical goals and conceal or confuse the moral issues. We must, therefore, be ever vigilant to use principled reasoning in the pursuit of ethical decision making."[24]

Practicing ethics isn't easy. Many individuals and organizations spend a lot of time talking about ethics and ways to teach employees to be ethical. But after all the talking, what happens? How is theory transformed into practice?

Before individuals or organizations proclaim themselves to be ethical, they should make ethics the foundation upon which their decisions and behavior are based.

CHAPTER FOUR

From Theory to Practice: The Business of Public Relations

In the fall of 1991, public relations professionals gathered at their annual convention in Phoenix, Arizona, to contemplate the future of their industry. The convention theme, "Credibility in an Incredible World," reflected the growing concern among practitioners about professional ethics.

That theme is particularly appropriate for a discussion of ethical business practices in public relations. The increasingly competitive climate in which firms operate—coupled with a society that rewards winning above all else—creates an environment in which acceptable behavior often is defined as doing "whatever it takes" to come out on top.[1]

Competitive pressures weigh heavily on decisions regarding the actions that are necessary for accomplishing organizational objectives.[2] Although recognizing the existence of ethical standards, practitioners too often are swayed to violate them for what are perceived to be the greater rewards of profit and position.[3]

Perhaps J.R. Ewing, the wealthy oil baron of the popular television show "Dallas," best described this "anything to win" philosophy when asked to explain his business success. "Once you've given up your ethics, the rest is a piece of cake," he said.[4]

It's tough to be good in a world where being bad apparently pays off.

In the long run, however, the payoff may be different. The definitive reward for the unprincipled, profit-driven practitioner may be loss of credibility, clients, and clout.

Public relations professionals know that a business will succeed only if it earns the trust and support of the public. As they so often counsel their clients, "before we can convince anyone that you are good, you have to be good."

With that in mind, the ethical standards by which public relations professionals measure their clients should be applied to their own business practices.

PROVIDING PROFESSIONAL SERVICES

Inherent in the definition of "professional" are the obligation and ability to provide expert, objective advice. Professionals who violate this duty often find themselves defending both legal and ethical claims of professional misconduct.

For professional services providers, malfeasance and incompetence rank high on the list of ethical concerns.[5]

Malfeasance simply means that services that should not be performed are performed. Lawyers file frivolous lawsuits. Doctors conduct unnecessary procedures. Public relations professionals execute campaigns they know will not be effective and implement programs that are not necessary.

Although there has been no formal reporting about the frequency of that last problem, it does illustrate an important ethical dilemma for public relations professionals. When a potential client requests services that may be either inappropriate or unnecessary, must the advisor subordinate his or her own interest to that of the client—and pass up the opportunity to make money?

Of course, the answer is clear. The professional status to which public relations practitioners have for so long aspired carries with it a special obligation to place service ahead of personal gain.[6]

In reality, however, mere knowledge that a competitor is more than willing to accept the proffered project or that this account will rank the firm higher than its toughest competitor may be enough to make a public relations counselor cross ethical boundaries and accept the account. Worse yet, other practitioners might readily accept, explaining that, for them, there is no ethical dilemma because all of their decisions are "bottom line"-based.[7]

An example of this problem is holding expensive, multicity news conferences at a client's behest, even though the retained public relations professional knows that another approach would be more appropriate for accomplishing the client's objectives.

The PRSA Code of Professional Standards deals indirectly with this issue in several articles, which require members to exemplify high standards of integrity and deal fairly with clients. The PRSA Counselors Academy's interpretations go a step further in precept 4: "It is incumbent on counselors to understand the requirements of their clients and to exert best efforts to satisfy those requirements by submitting realistic proposals on performance, cost and schedule."

Article 1 of the general PRSA Code also requires that "a member shall conduct his or her life in accord with the public interest." Certainly it is not in either the client's or the public's interest for unscrupulous professionals to provide needless services.

INCOMPETENCE

The "bottom line" mentality may also be blamed for the offering of public relations services by unqualified practitioners. The lucrative nature of the public relations industry has attracted a growing number of professionals who claim the title "public relations counselor" with no experience or education to back it up. Additionally, the potential for increased billings has persuaded some experienced counselors to expand their services into areas they know little about.

"Rainmakers" play a big role in public relations, just as they do in other professional services industries. "Selling the sizzle without the steak" is, unfortunately, a familiar phrase among public relations practitioners.

A 1992 "Issues and Trends" report by the PRSA Counselors Academy pointed out that "a public relations firm does not absolutely need to have a skill set or service. It need only convince a client that it has them and be able to deliver at some point, if the firm wishes to keep the client."[8] Continuing, the report notes that "the key to value-added for prospective clients is perception, and perception is often shaped by superior salesmanship. That is why 'rainmakers' will continue to drive the industry and why competition among public relations firms will continue to be fierce."[9]

True enough, but these statements do not speak to the ethics of offering skills one does not possess. Most would agree that it is unethical for professionals to risk harm to clients and to jeopardize public confidence in the industry by selling services they are not qualified to provide.

The PRSA Code addresses this issue only in the Official Interpretations of the Code as It Applies to Political and Financial Public Relations. Members in these areas are required to be knowledgeable about the laws and regulations that govern political and financial activities and to seek appropriate counsel when necessary.

A similar rule requiring practitioners to possess the capabilities they offer should be applied across the board for all areas of practice. Practitioners would not be prohibited from offering services in unfamiliar areas; they would merely be required to retain competent associates to assist in the representation. For their counterparts in law and other professions, that is standard practice.

The practitioner who operates on the "greed is good" theory might thoughtfully reconsider his or her obligation both to clients and to the public relations profession. The responsibility is to help a client make a decision that appropriately meets the needs of the client and, in doing so, serves the public interest and advances the industry's goals.

SOLICITATION OF CLIENTS

Solicitation of clients is the issue that creates the most enmity among public relations counselors. Some firms follow the philosophy of "all's fair in love, war, and public relations." Others take a more honorable approach in their efforts to expand their client base.

Article 14 of the PRSA Code of Professional Standards states: "A member shall not intentionally damage the professional reputation or practice of another practitioner." This article is interpreted to include stealing other members' clients—conduct that was explicitly prohibited in earlier versions of the code.

In 1977, the society amended the code to eliminate the encroachment provision in response to concerns that the statement could be perceived as promoting restraint of trade. According to PRSA, the society's stance on the issue did not change, however, and has always "been the same as that of many other professions, most of whose members do not, as a matter of principle, raid or pirate others' clients."[10]

Examples of this can easily be found in the marketing materials of Realtors and other professional services providers. Direct-mail pieces explicitly state that if the potential client is already working with another provider, the contact should not be regarded as an attempt to solicit business.

Today, the PRSA Code Interpretation of article 14 states: "Blind solicitation, on its face, is not prohibited by the Code. However, if the customer list were improperly obtained, or if the solicitation contained references reflecting adversely on the quality of current services, a complaint might be justified."

Public relations professionals walk a fine line in staying on the right side of this issue. A popular example involves the indirect solicitation of a competitor's client by a leading agency executive.

A CEO of one of the world's largest public relations firms writes in his book: "I routinely make a point of calling on the CEOs of my competitors' largest accounts with useful information. The visit takes no more than thirty minutes; the recovery time for my competitors is generally two to three days."[11]

In responding to such behavior, industry leader John Budd says, "This particular CEO, I am sure, does not disparage his competitor nor, I doubt, does he even mention the worthy by name. But he knows, as you and I do, that is close to the edge, and certainly in violation of the 'spirit' if not the legal aspects of the code he professes to endorse."[12]

The strength of a code of ethics, of course, lies in self-regulation by members. "Ethical rules do not resolve ethical dilemmas nor create ethical practitioners," notes Budd.[13]

In practice, perhaps the best rule to guide professionals on this issue is a familiar one: Do unto others as you would have them do unto you.

NOT GUARANTEEING RESULTS

The PRSA Code of Professional Standards caught the attention of the Federal Trade Commission (FTC) in 1977 because of a provision prohibiting members from charging fees contingent on specified results. The FTC objected to the provision as a violation of federal antitrust law against price-fixing.[14]

PRSA's response was to lift the ban on contingency fees and to allow fee structures based on outcome.

Article 9 now reads: "A member shall not guarantee the achievement of specified results beyond the member's direct control." The interpretation explains further: "The Code paragraph, in effect, prohibits misleading a client or employer as to what professional public relations can accomplish. It does not prohibit guarantees of quality of service. But it does prohibit guaranteeing specific results which, by their very nature, cannot be guaranteed because they are not subject to the member's control. As an example, a guarantee that a news release will appear specifically in a particular publication would be prohibited. This paragraph should not be interpreted as prohibiting contingency fees."

This article has commanded a lot of attention in today's competitive marketplace. Just how far can a practitioner go in predicting outcome?

Most practitioners would agree that overpromising simply to beat out a competitor is bad business. Not only do false promises ensure no repeat customers, but they also establish expectations that if unmet could result in legal liability.

Presenting results of past programs is one acceptable way to indicate capabilities. Track records speak for themselves. However, if circumstances are different—and they always are—it is never safe to guarantee that past successes can be repeated.

Gaining client agreement on the goals and strategies of a program and the level of service to be provided is a better approach to gaining and keeping clients. Research studies show that client decisions to hire and retain professional services firms are primarily based on the quality of service provided—rather than merely on potential results.

With specific regard to contingency fees, many professionals believe that working on a contingency basis is unethical even though no longer prohibited by the code. For them, basing payment on specified results comes too close to a guarantee of results.

For those who choose to accept a contingency fee structure, potential problems should be anticipated and addressed up front. Let's say a practitioner is approached by a CEO who seeks to reestablish herself as a leader in her industry. She agrees to pay $50,000 if the firm is successful in getting her picture on the cover of the industry's most prestigious magazine. Otherwise, no fee. Any problem?

By the way, what happens if the picture runs under the headline, "The Downfall of a CEO"?

Some U.S. practitioners consider their British counterparts' approach to this issue most appropriate. The British Institute of Public Relations' Code of Professional Conduct explicitly prohibits contingency fees and states that public relations "practitioners should be paid for their effort and expertise—their time according to its value—not results. . . ."[15]

CONTROVERSIAL ACCOUNTS

Increasing recognition of the power and influence of public relations has fueled concern about the potential misuse of public relations and has led the industry to examine its advocacy role.[16] Specifically, the questions debated are (1) which clients and what causes are ethically acceptable, and (2) are any potential clients personæ non grata?

Unfortunately for practitioners, there is much controversy and little guidance from the industry regarding ethical boundaries on this issue. The code's only reference to choice of clients appears in a special section for those involved in political public relations. The PRSA Counselors Academy's interpretations simply state that "Counselors have an overriding responsibility to carefully balance public interests with those of their clients, and to place both interests above their own."

Diverse and emotional views have been expressed on the issue of representation. One theory is that such decisions should be left to the sole discretion of individual practitioners, who have the right to decide what causes and institutions are worthy of representation.[17] Another perspective is that the institutions "beyond the point of rehabilitation" are indefensible.[18]

Notwithstanding one's moral stance on debatable issues and the willingness of practitioners to assume individual responsibility for supporting selected causes, the fact is that the entire industry suffers when firms take on bad clients. For that reason, the topic merits discussion.

The most visible representation controversies have involved the international firm Hill and Knowlton, which first became the target of harsh criticism for its representation of the United States Catholic Conference. The Catholic bishops retained the agency in 1991 to conduct an antiabortion campaign.[19]

Since that time, Hill and Knowlton has found itself embroiled in more public controversy for representing unpopular clients. For example, the firm took on Citizens for a Free Kuwait (discussed in Chapter Seven), the controversial Bank of Credit and Commerce International, and the Church of Scientology.

Hill and Knowlton representatives have defended the representation of these clients both by citing the First Amendment and by suggesting that critics were upset simply because they did not agree with the specific causes represented.[20]

Whether right or wrong, however, Hill and Knowlton's representation of these clients—and news reports of the high price tags attached to that representation—cast negative shadows on the public relations industry and focused national media attention on questions regarding whether and how such clients should be handled.[21]

Should public relations professionals be viewed much like lawyers, who have a professional obligation to zealously represent their clients even if they disagree with what their clients are doing (or have done in the past)? Or should public relations professionals be held accountable both personally and professionally for the position they assume in the representation of clients and their causes?

These tough questions have no easy answers. The simplest solution to this ethical quandary would be to accept the "attorney advocate" model often proposed to explain the role of the public relations professional.[22] Applying this model, public relations professionals, like attorneys, could represent any client with no fear of retribution since the client's beliefs or character could not be attributed to the individual practitioner.[23]

The PRSA Code provides some support for this approach in the Official Interpretation of the Code as It Applies to Political Public Relations. The precepts state that in the practice of political public relations, "members may serve their employer or client

without necessarily having attributed to them the character, reputation or beliefs of those they serve."

On the other hand, a compelling argument could be made that,
because these statements apply only to "political" public relations,
code drafters had no intention for such reasoning to be applied in
other circumstances.

This "attorney" model—which many practitioners cling to in
defense of their representation of questionable clients—has other
shortcomings. Although both public relations and legal counselors
serve as organizational advocates, the public relations professional's role is far more expansive than that of the attorney, who
must simply present his or her client's case in the court of law as a
disassociated representative.[24]

Public relations professionals who serve as the "social conscience" of their organizations act as intermediaries between organizations and their publics in a role that requires adherence to public
service and social responsibility.[25] The practitioner cannot in good
faith (and ethically) represent an organization involved in bad deeds.

Ironically, one of the founding partners of Hill and Knowlton
wrote thirty years ago that "the greatest hope for the future of public relations counseling lies in . . . establishing ethical standards and
sound practices . . . the examples set by the leading firms will prove
of major importance in achieving desired public recognition."[26]

The chairman of Edelman Public Relations Worldwide echoes
these thoughts today and calls for public relations professionals to
maintain high standards in judging who will be represented and
what the firm will do for them. "Let's not allow greed to blur our
vision and commitment to do the right thing, to work for the right
kind of people and to counsel them in the first direction," he says.[27]

Unfortunately, Edelman neglects to define "right," just as the
industry has neglected to define "bad." The complex nature of this
issue seems to preclude resolution by either consensus or reliance
on a code of ethics. Thus, the choice of client, cause, or issue falls
to the individual practitioner.

Those who are in the position of making these difficult choices
should consider that although they alone will bear responsibility for
their decisions, the entire industry will be held accountable for their
actions.

CONFLICTS OF INTEREST

Article 10 of the PRSA Code requires that members "not represent conflicting or competing interests without the express consent of those concerned, given after a full disclosure of facts." For agency professionals, this provision holds particular significance.

According to the authors of *Public Relations: The Necessary Art*, "one of the most difficult aspects of conflicts of interest is recognizing them and admitting they exist."[28] The practitioner must be constantly attuned to changing circumstances that could create conflicts.

Consider, for example, the agency that represents both a health care services provider and a pharmaceutical products retail chain. At the outset, no conflicts are there. When the health care company decides to expand its operations to include in-house pharmacies, however, a direct conflict is created.

Even if clients agree to continuing representation in conflict situations, the agency must be aware of subtle dangers that must be avoided. For example, "unconscious favoritism, the unwitting use of confidential client information for the benefit of a competitor and the potential for a lesser creative effort for one client" are issues of concern.[29] The PRSA Code's article 13 states that a "member shall scrupulously safeguard the confidences and privacy rights of present, former, and prospective clients or employers."

Conflict of interest issues also involve situations in which a professional is asked to represent a cause that he or she personally opposes. Consider the dilemma of a young professional who, upon graduation, goes to work for the Office of Cancer Communications in the National Institutes of Health. Her job involves assisting the director of a national cancer awareness program in developing a campaign to educate Americans about ways to reduce their risks of getting cancer. When she leaves the institute and moves to another city (where the job market is tight), the only job offer she receives is with an agency that represents a tobacco company. Although she is strongly opposed to the promotion and sale of tobacco products, she needs a job. What should she do? If she accepts, will she be able to provide competent representation for this client? Will she be able to sleep at night?

This scenario illustrates the importance of considering all the loyalties involved in public relations work. How should duties to self, client, and the public be prioritized in such situations? Does article 11 of the PRSA Code help resolve the dilemma?

Staff professionals also confront conflict of interest issues. Consider the corporate director of public relations who loves the arts and is actively involved in the nonprofit arts community. The director is also asked to serve as a free-lance campaign director for the local theatre's annual fund-raising drive. It is a paid position, and all the work will be done after office hours. Any problems?

Professionals who face conflict of interest dilemmas must first recognize all the interests involved and then abide by a "full disclosure" policy. Only when all parties are apprised about potential conflicts can informed ethical decisions be reached.

NONPROFIT PUBLIC RELATIONS

"The nonprofit world doesn't have much better luck than corporate America when it comes to figuring out how to monitor ethics," according to a recent *Wall Street Journal* article.[30] *Time* followed close behind with an article noting that although the vast majority of charities are well run and dedicated to helping others, "as their numbers and size have increased, they have attracted a rising number of swindlers, creative bookkeepers and highly paid executives."[31]

Examples of misconduct abound, always beginning with the United Way scandal in which the national president was forced to resign after being charged with misuse of funds. Accusations against other organizations have ranged from deceptive fund-raising strategies to blatant mismanagement. Even the Girl Scouts have experienced problems with disgruntled volunteers who say local troops don't see enough of the profits from the annual cookie sale.[32]

Such criticism reflects a declining public trust in and an increasing demand for accountability in nonprofit organizations. Contributors and other supporters are questioning how funds are spent and demanding documented responses. Journalist Rayna Skolnik notes that people want to know what the organization's objectives are and why those objectives are worthwhile. "And, ultimately, they want proof that the objectives actually are being achieved using their dollars."[33]

Since nonprofit organizations depend on public confidence to remain viable, rebuilding credibility with constituents is critical. This requires both reactive programs in the sense of being responsive to public inquiries and proactive programs in the sense of developing campaigns to reestablish positive relationships with donors, volunteers, and other supporters.

Looking at nonprofits from a theoretical perspective, few people would suggest that the ends sought could be construed as unethical. It is the means, then, that demand attention. Specific strategies and tactics, operating policies and procedures, and whether, in fact, stated goals are reached, must be examined. Both the public's right to know and the rights of those who support organizational activities must be considered.

Notwithstanding the ethical lapses that have occurred in the nonprofit area, it is important to also consider other reasons that people question what they see as unethical behavior. For example, a lack of understanding can often lead to negative attitudes. Arthur Smith, director of public relations for Volunteers of America, suggests that much of the concern with the ethics of nonprofits is based on misperceptions of how these organizations operate. "The media and public don't understand the nonprofit sector," he says. "We need to tell our story."[34]

GLOBAL ETHICS

Globalization has presented new ethical challenges for U.S. professionals who must apply Americanized codes of ethics in foreign markets. For public relations practitioners who are charged with establishing a client's positive presence throughout the world, the challenge is particularly daunting.

As the number of multinational firms increases, companies and nations will become more interdependent and will be forced to work together for mutual benefit.[35] Public relations practitioners would be wise to consider the ethical choices they will face in the global market.

Practitioners who have tried to transplant American ethics into foreign cultures have quickly learned that people of different backgrounds and training approach situations with different value systems and standards of performance. What is illegal in one market may be acceptable and widespread in others.[36]

For example, in some countries payments to customs officials to move goods across borders may be routine practice, much like tipping service workers in the United States. In other places, communications professionals may "charge" journalists for information provided.[37]

The issue of global ethics is not always a question of a country's values being right or wrong, or better or worse than another's. Although corrupt practices do occur, customs of other nations are not necessarily bad just because they are different.

The international practitioner must be sensitive to social, cultural, and other differences that determine the context in which moral dilemmas arise.[38] In discussing ethical relativism, the authors of *Communication Ethics* suggest that a compelling argument can be made to follow the old adage "When in Rome, do as the Romans do." "History strongly suggests that someday we will view some of our present practices as ethically flawed . . . [one] should not automatically assume that he or she understands another society's practices well enough to criticize them, let alone attempt to change them."[39]

Kent Hodgson, author of *A Rock and a Hard Place: Making Ethical Business Decisions When the Choices are Tough*, suggests that attempts to impose one's values on others can "destroy any sense of cooperation based on mutual trust and goodwill. . . . While different from yours and mine in many ways, the cultures and customs of other countries are not beyond a working spirit of what we both would call, in our own ways, cooperation and shared moral responsibility."[40]

Applying that spirit to practice, however, can present problems. Joyce Wouters points out some of the practical difficulties of operating in foreign territory in *International Public Relations*. "In some cultures, the giving and receiving of monetary gifts or even tangible gifts of some value is an accepted and legal practice in circumstances that would be interpreted in the United States as bribery; often, there is no stigma attached to such a practice and obedience to custom is important in indicating one's sincerity or loyalty."[41]

Participating in corrupt activities has its price, however. Barbara Burns, a public relations consultant and member of the board of directors of the International Public Relations Association, has noted that in certain countries it is not unusual for public relations professionals to pay journalists to have favorable stories for clients placed in publications. "But everyone knows which publications these are—so placement is not so valuable to the client," Burns said. "And if you start paying off, it undermines your credibility, and finally your business."[42]

Practitioners operating abroad should first ensure that they and their clients are aware of and in compliance with the laws that affect business practices in foreign countries. The U.S. Foreign Corrupt Practices Act is of particular importance. This act makes it a crime for U.S. companies to pay officials of foreign governments for assistance in obtaining business.[43]

The act, which was intended to eliminate corrupt practices of U.S. multinationals, distinguishes illegal "bribes" from legal "gratuities" that can be paid to expedite routine government activities such as the provision of visas or the inspection of goods. Although it has been criticized as an attempt by the United States to "export its morality," the act also has been acknowledged as the impetus for improvements in company policies regarding international business dealings.[44]

Business scholars have suggested that improvements in foreign government operations may have to originate with American companies. A professor at the University of Pennsylvania's Wharton School has noted that if American companies continue to participate in corrupt practices, then a government has no incentive to be efficient. On the other hand, suggests the professor, if companies pressure governments to clean up their acts, the system might change.[45]

Public Relations Professor Dean Kruckeberg suggests that developing an international code of ethics for public relations professionals would also improve the ethical climate of the global market. Although he notes that codes of ethics are not enough, "a thoughtfully constructed code based on various theories of moral philosophy as applied to public relations *as a profession* with a common body of knowledge and agreed-upon standards of behavior is a logical universal beginning. Exposing transnational corporations to yet another profession's code of ethics in the deliberation of its policies and actions would certainly contribute additional valuable insights beneficial to transnational corporate policymaking."[46]

The PRSA Code makes no specific reference to practice in foreign locations. Some guidance can be found, however, in the Code of Athens adopted by the International Public Relations Association in 1965 and followed by public relations professionals in more than seventy countries.

Emphasizing human rights, the behavior of public relations practitioners, and the image of the profession, the Code of Athens has been recognized for its success in establishing ethical standards that are universally acceptable.[47] An outline of the code's principles follows:

> A member shall endeavor to comply with the following requirements:
>
> 1. To contribute to the achievement of the moral and cultural conditions enabling human beings to reach their full stature and enjoy the indefeasible rights to which they are entitled under the Universal Declaration of Human Rights.
>
> 2. To establish communication patterns and channels that, by fostering the free flow of essential information, will make each member of the society in which he lives feel that he is being informed, and also give him awareness of his own personal involvement and responsibility, and of his solidarity with other members.
>
> 3. To bear in mind that, because of the relationship between his profession and the public, his conduct—even in private—will have an impact on the way in which the profession as a whole is appraised.
>
> 4. To respect, in the course of his professional duties, the moral principles and rules of the Universal Declaration of Human Rights.
>
> 5. To pay due regard to, and uphold, human dignity, and to recognize the right of each individual to judge for himself.
>
> 6. To encourage the moral, psychological, and intellectual conditions for dialogue in its true sense, and to recognize the right of the parties involved to state their case and express their views.

A member shall undertake:

7. To conduct himself always and in all circumstances in such a manner as to deserve and secure the confidence of those with whom he comes into contact.

8. To act, in all circumstances, in such a manner as to take account of the respective interests of the parties involved: both the interests of the organization that he serves and the interests of the public concerned.

9. To carry out his duties with integrity, avoiding language likely to lead to ambiguity or misunderstanding, and to maintain loyalty to his clients or employers, whether past or present.

A member shall refrain from:

10. Subordinating the truth to other requirements.

11. Circulating information that is not based on established and ascertainable facts.

12. Taking part in any venture or undertaking that is unethical or dishonest or capable of impairing human dignity and integrity.

13. Using any "manipulative" methods or techniques designed to create subconscious motivation that the individual cannot control of his own free will and so cannot be held accountable for the action taken on them.

These guidelines sound familiar. The underlying principles of honesty, integrity, and respect are also found in the PRSA Code of Professional Standards. The challenge of global ethics—as at home—is incorporating them into business practices.

CHAPTER FIVE

Truth as Ethical Imperative

"Does the word 'lie' actually mean anything any more? In one sense, everyone lies, but in another sense, no one does, because no one knows what's true—it's whatever makes you look good."[1]

That bit of confused and confusing pragmatism was offered by a public relations practitioner working for one of America's ten largest corporations. It underscores the perpetual difficulty of finding an answer to one of the oldest questions: What is truth?

The PRSA Code of Professional Standards grapples with this issue. Article 3 states: "A member shall adhere to truth and accuracy and to generally accepted standards of good taste." Article 7 says: "A member shall not intentionally communicate false or misleading information."

In researching public relations professionals' attitudes about these standards, Professor Marvin Olasky found various definitions of "truth and accuracy." One manager advocated "fact accuracy" but claimed that still left room for "professional manipulation of impression." He told Olasky: "I don't lie. I've never lied. There's a fine line sometimes, but I've never had data in front of me and read off the wrong numbers to a reporter." Another public relations manager said that rigid adherence to truth was not as important as loyalty to your bosses. "You have to let top executives know you'll support them in whatever they do. You'll lie for them, you'll cheat for them, you'll cover up for them. Doing whatever it takes to get the job done (is) all in an honest day's work."[2]

The honesty of such a day's work is certainly debatable. Fortunately, that practitioner's attitude about the truth is, presumably, as atypical as it is incompatible with the PRSA Code. It does, however, illustrate the dynamic tension that exists between ethical standards and rough-and-tumble business practices.

Definitions of "truth" range along a broad spectrum. At one end is "absolute truth"; at the other is the cavalier "tell the truth when it happens to be convenient, and don't be afraid to embellish it along the way." As a practical matter, the boundary between ethically acceptable and unacceptable falls in between, closer to the former than the latter, but not at the farthest point on that spectrum.

Taking an absolutist position about truth might seem to be the most ethical approach, but certainty about what is true is often elusive. Opinion, completeness of information, interpretation, and perception influence the shaping of truth.

For example, in response to a media inquiry, should the public relations professional merely answer the questions asked (which might lead to a misleading story) or volunteer additional information? In his book *The Credibility Factor*, Lee Baker quotes public relations counselor Joe Epley about this issue: "I don't think that the spirit of openness in public relations is like a confessional at a Baptist revival, where one gets up and spills his guts to everyone to cleanse his soul. Where is the line that says enough is enough? That's one of the biggest challenges we as practitioners have to find; and, when we come to that line, and there is still a question, we should err on the side of more disclosure. There can . . . be no compromise with honesty."[3]

Even statistics, which supposedly don't lie, are only stepping-stones on the path toward truth. The "spin" put on numbers or on any other facts may affect perceptions of their meaning. Particularly when the information is about an event in progress or about something yet to happen, the truthfulness of that information often depends on the eye of the beholder.

Consider this example:

An accident at a manufacturing company's plant produces a large chemical spill. The company's public relations office releases a statement saying the firm's engineers have determined that no environmental damage will occur.

Is that the truth? Assume that the engineers believe their judgment to be sound. That doesn't make it true. Other environmental experts then survey the situation and predict that serious damage will result. Both sides offer evidence to support their claims. Is one side lying and the other telling the truth? Not necessarily. Both might be good-faith statements, based on truth.

Should the company's public relations practitioners include in the news release a note about the differing viewpoints? Would that addition make their position truer or just more confusing? And what about their obligation to present their company in the best possible light? If they believe their engineers' statement to be true—or at least as true as the other experts' appraisal—shouldn't the news release simply present the company's point of view?

In such instances, often no one knows for certain what the absolute truth is. No one is being purposely deceitful; the information being offered is fundamentally—if not "absolutely"—truthful. As Alice said in *Through the Looking Glass*, "The question is whether you *can* make words mean so many different things."

A parallel exists in journalism. News organizations know that if they wait to determine the absolute truth about most stories, they will end up publishing monthly at best. So they balance their need to be accurate with their need to deliver news promptly. One standard that some employ is to settle for "the best obtainable version" of the truth. The ethical challenge is to set reasonable-yet-rigorous standards for "best obtainable."

For instance, how many corroborating sources should be required to back up the primary source to ensure that the resulting news story is the best obtainable version? One? Five? Twenty?

Precise standards may vary according to the importance of the story and the difficulty in getting information. For example, suppose a reporter is investigating allegations about wrongdoing by an elected official. The principal source demands confidentiality—no mention of his name in the published story. Some news organizations might require at least two corroborating sources before the original information is printed. This would help prevent the source from using anonymity to make unfounded charges. Perhaps further corroboration should be required; what if all three informants are wrong? But most journalists would probably consider the use of one original and two supporting sources to be sufficient to meet the standard of publishing the best obtainable version of the truth.

Both journalists and public relations professionals have an ethical "duty to inquire" about the truthfulness of the information they publish.

David Drobis, PRSA Fellow and chairman and CEO of Ketchum Public Relations Worldwide, says this duty requires public relations professionals to be good reporters. "Externally, journalists play the role of the devil's advocate, putting company statements, facts and positions to the test of public opinion. Internally, public relations practitioners should, to some extent, mimic the role of the media and the public, testing and refining the company's position by challenging it."[4]

According to Drobis, it is incumbent on public relations professionals to ask tough questions in an effort to develop suitable responses to inquiries and concerns from a variety of audiences. The best policy for all, he says, is to "work on the assumption that every business decision that is made will become public knowledge and will influence the company's reputation."[5]

Drobis also notes that whether the disclosure of incomplete or conflicting information is the result of negligence or a deliberate attempt to mislead the public, the result is the same—the reputation of the company suffers damage. "With so much at stake, it pays for managers and public relations practitioners to fully understand their duty to inquire and appreciate the role this responsibility plays in advancing the organizations they represent."[6]

PUFFERY AND ITS LIMITS

At the root of truth is solid, unadorned fact. Relying on fact, writes Charles Steinberg, has its value: "Apart from ethical considerations, facts are useful in public relations because, in the long run, they are less troublesome and more valid. They tend to solidify the base of operations for the future, both with mass media and the public." But Steinberg also notes: "Each individual within a public or group accepts or rejects the message in terms of his own value judgments and orientation. That is why a bald telling of the facts will not always be successful in practice."[7]

That premise leads to the use of puffery—enlarging truth and remolding fact to serve the information disseminator's purpose. Given that truth has many variations, to what extent is puffery ethically permissible? At what point does truth become so exaggerated or reworked that it is transformed into falsehood?

Finding that precise boundary is extremely difficult. If truth-telling is to go beyond technical accuracy and reach the level of trustworthiness,[8] then even providing information that is true but one-sided may be unacceptable. On the other hand, most people are not wholly naive. Puffery is often assumed, and its presence is factored into decisions about the overall credibility of a message. The advertising field provides good examples of how puffery is used to enhance the purported attributes of products and services.

In public relations, *how* puffery is used—rather than *whether* it is used—is the crucial matter. The selection of information and the emphasis placed on it may constitute puffery.

Consider this hypothetical case. You are public relations director for Behemoth, Inc., an automobile manufacturer. Your new model, the Aristocrat, will be in dealers' showrooms within a few weeks. Behemoth has hired an independent consumer-testing service to evaluate the Aristocrat. The service's report, available only to Behemoth executives, is decidedly mixed. It praises the Aristocrat's styling and acceleration, but it sharply criticizes its low gas mileage and its failure to include various safety features. You issue a news release, quoting extensively from the report's favorable passages but making no mention of the criticisms.

Is that ethical? Nothing in your release is untrue, but by being so selective you have exaggerated the Aristocrat's positive attributes.

Suppose you also say in your news release, "Respected automobile industry experts predict that the Aristocrat will undoubtedly be the finest car on the road." The release doesn't mention that those "experts" all are Behemoth executives. Claiming that the Aristocrat will be the "finest car on the road" is a matter of opinion, but given the consumer service's test results, it is likely to be an opinion shared by few.

Is this exaggeration acceptable? It is "true," in the sense that the statement was made by the Behemoth executives, but this is a marginal kind of truth.

Again, one defense of puffery is that the public and the news media expect it and balance the claims with a dose of skepticism and independent investigation. But some people are more gullible than others. The public relations practitioner might say: "That's not my problem." Or, in cases in which the public relations information is relayed by news media, the practitioner might argue that journalists assume some responsibility for verifying claims and soliciting different views before delivering the information to the public.

All this may seem to constitute a formidable defense for the public relations practitioner's use of puffery. But it also smacks of buckpassing—a contention that determining the truth is someone else's responsibility.

Legally, the First Amendment's free speech guarantee protects exaggerations such as those in the Aristocrat case. But ethically, puffery is on flimsier ground. Practitioners must decide for themselves how far they will stretch the limits of truthfulness, but while doing so they should keep in mind that honesty remains a keystone of ethics. Ethical boundaries do exist. (Those who work for publicly held corporations also have a *legal* duty to comply with securities laws that require companies to report accurately *all* information that might be important to investors.)

QUOTES—REAL AND INVENTED

An indispensable part of a news release is the quotation from an authoritative figure that states the essence of the employer's/client's position. "Putting quote marks around ideas and attributing them to a spokesperson enables you to state your organization's view unabashedly and with vigor. . . . It is the responsibility of the public relations people to sift through the opinions, ideas, statements, records, and reports of management, then *create* the neat pithy quotes that will appear in the news release."[9]

As this description of the drafting process indicates, the quotes appearing in press releases often have not been actually spoken by the person to whom they are attributed. This is not unlike the way the president of the United States relies on the work of a White House speech writer. The speech is the president's message incorporating the president's ideas. Depending on its quality it will be soon forgotten or long remembered as the president's. All this, even though much of the wording and perhaps even rhetorical style has been crafted by someone else.

The ethical requirements of this practice are based not on how or by whom the quotes are created, but on the accuracy of the statements. The quotes should correctly depict the quoted person's views, as well as define the position of the institution he or she represents.

PLAGIARISM

The ethical rule about plagiarism is simple: Don't do it.

Using the words of others and passing them off *as your own* is stealing. Assembling a quote, as discussed above, is not plagiarism when it is authorized. Article 6 of the PRSA Code requires that practitioners give "credit for ideas and words borrowed from others."

Whenever the words of others are used, they should be attributed unless permission that this need not be done has been granted. For example, if a corporate officer has stated her company's position about a matter, the public relations person might transform those words into a statement attributed not to the original speaker but to someone else or to the institution collectively. That is fine, as long as it is done with her permission.

Public relations professionals—like journalists and others—must be careful to avoid even inadvertent plagiarism. In particular, note-taking should be done meticulously so that when the notes are used their sources can be properly credited.

Failure to do this can cause great harm. For instance, Senator Joe Biden's 1988 presidential campaign was severely damaged when people learned that his standard stump speech borrowed extensively—without attribution—from the speeches of British politician Neil Kinnock. When the news media charged Biden with plagiarism, voters' opinions of his honesty plummeted.

This is a good object lesson for all those who work with the words of others. Plagiarism is wrong, and when it is found out the plagiarizer—and those he or she represents—are likely to be treated harshly.

DISINFORMATION

Beyond one-sidedness and exaggeration is disinformation—purposeful use of information known to be basically untrue.

Ponder your actions as a public relations practitioner in this hypothetical case. You have been hired by the owner of a well-known and extremely profitable hotel that has been the subject of negative news stories about the owner's allegedly unfair treatment of the hotel's maids and porters. The workers' discontent has led to union picketing at the hotel and still more unfavorable news coverage. You fail to come up with positive story ideas that reporters are likely to use, so you decide to try to neutralize the union efforts. The leader of this hotel workers' union was briefly investigated five years ago by federal agents looking into ties between unions and organized crime. No charges were ever filed against the union leader, and he was not investigated further.

Nevertheless, you mention to several reporters and editors that you have "heard that this union guy was being investigated not too long ago by the feds. Word on the street is that he's got mob ties." Several subsequent news stories about problems at the hotel mention the investigation. This takes some heat off your client. Instead of being an oppressor of workers, he now will seem to some news consumers as possibly being a victim of mobsters.

You knew there was no solid evidence of wrongdoing by the labor leader, but you used the existence of the investigation and gossip to create a smoke screen, hoping to offset some of the negative coverage of your client. Is this unethical use of disinformation, for which you should be faulted? Or is it merely dissemination of technically accurate, if extraneous, information that the reporters improperly overplayed? Should *misleading* information—even if technically correct—be one of the tools that a public relations professional uses on behalf of a client?

The PRSA Code would seem to answer these questions with its requirement of adherence to truth and accuracy. The code also bars knowingly disseminating "misleading information." Use of disinformation falls well short of meeting this standard.

Worth noting is that among the principal purveyors of disinformation are governments and intelligence agencies trying to lead their adversaries astray. For instance, during the Cold War the U.S. Department of Defense might have released figures about American defense capabilities that Pentagon officials knew to be false, hoping that Soviet analysts would be misled by them. The Soviet Union played the same game. But what is a common tactic in the geopolitical wilderness of mirrors is not necessarily proper in public relations practice.

H.J. Dalton, Jr., a former PRSA president and a retired Air Force brigadier general, has said, "I cannot accept or condone disinformation as a public relations tactic in the corporate world." The company that uses such a ploy, he says, "risks losing the confidence of all its publics."[10]

The fallback position for public relations practitioners such as the one representing the hotel owner is that responsibility to the client is more important than niceties about the limits of truth-stretching. That pseudo-noble posture, however, is tantamount to a justification of ethical anarchy. Virtually any measure—certainly any legal measure—could be rationalized as acceptable because it serves a client's interests. To claim that this end justifies the means is dangerously facile philosophizing.

CORRECTING ERRORS

Even when following ethically rigorous standards about accuracy, a public relations practitioner might inadvertently communicate erroneous information. Given the volume of material that is generated in public relations efforts, some slipups are bound to happen.

But inevitability is merely an explanation, not a justification. The PRSA Code's article 5 requires a member to "act promptly to correct erroneous communications for which he or she is responsible."

Similarly, even if the mistake has been transmitted by a medium outside the control of the public relations professional (such as a news organization), the obligation to accuracy does not shift. Once an error has been detected, it should be corrected as promptly and thoroughly as possible. The goal is to offset any damage that the mistake may have caused.

The obligation to correct is owed to various affected parties. The person or organization about whom or which the error was made is at the top of the list. The public that received the false information also deserves the corrected version. And whoever made the error will be well served by acknowledging it. Such forthrightness will help preserve long-term credibility.

Among the issues to consider when making a correction are these:

- Timeliness. As soon as the error is discovered, make every effort to gather and disseminate correct information. Sometimes this can be done almost instantly after the mistake has been made, but sometimes the error is not discovered and accurate information not acquired until weeks, months, or even years later.

"As soon as possible" remains the guiding principle, regardless of how soon that is.

- Clarity. Often errors arise from failure to state the issue at hand clearly. An incomplete statement or poorly written passage might seem erroneous to a reasonable consumer of the information. Sometimes a correction is really more a clarification than a substantive alteration of the original material.

- Remedial effect. Perhaps the mistake had little or no effect, but the correction should be written and disseminated based on the assumption that people have been misled and may have acted because of the error. Most errors in public relations work are "honest mistakes," and intent to cause harm is rarely an issue when inaccuracies occur. But the intent is less important than the result. Even if no legal liability is incurred, the ethical obligation is to right the wrong.

The following hypothetical case illustrates how these issues might arise.

You are public relations director for Hardcore Steel Company. Hardcore has quietly orchestrated the acquisition of longtime competitor Neverbend Steel Corporation. Both are publicly held companies with stock traded on the New York Stock Exchange. You issue a news release that says in part: "As one element of the acquisition, Hardcore will pay company chairman Joseph Neverbend $10 million and will pay Neverbend shareholders $5 per share for their stock. Mr. Neverbend says, 'This is a wonderful deal for me and for all Neverbend shareholders.'"

That sounds fine. But Hardcore's actual offer to Neverbend stockholders is $50 per share, which is slightly more than the stock's present worth. If the deal went through based on a $5-per-share valuation, it would be a disaster for Neverbend's investors.

When this release reaches the public through the news media, Neverbend shareholders might panic and try to sell their holdings immediately. Also, Mr. Neverbend appears to be gloating about his good fortune while his investors suffer. His reputation will be severely damaged.

The reason for the mistake doesn't matter. Whether it was caused by bad information from those involved in the acquisition, by a typographical error in the news release, or by anything else is beside the point. Also irrelevant is sloppy fact-checking by news organizations that reported the information. Whatever the reason, the damage has been done.

Perhaps the stock exchange will temporarily suspend trading in Neverbend (and probably Hardcore, too). And assume that securities regulations will come into play to bring the accurate information to light. But regardless of legal or other external requirements, the public relations director's responsibility is to issue a release *immediately* that corrects the first material. But that is unlikely to affect the public response to the first release. So, to offset damage, the public relations strategy should include extraordinary efforts, such as these:

- Telephone calls, faxes, and other measures to all news organizations that received the original release. These messages should stress the urgency of prominently publishing the new, correct information.
- Very explicit description of the real terms of the buyout. Rather than repeating the original release copy with just the dollar figure corrected, this second release should make certain that news organizations get the correct acquisition data. At this stage, precise information is what matters most.
- Other measures to counteract damage that has been done. This may involve purchasing advertisements in newspapers and newscasts to make certain that all investors and other interested persons know the truth about the stock price. Also, Mr. Neverbend's position needs to be clarified. He was praising the offer of $50 per share, which *is* a "wonderful deal" for his shareholders.

In this case, all this remedial action is the product of an apparently small error—one digit in a number. But the harm done was severe, and the efforts to correct should be thorough and unstinting.

DIFFERENT PUBLICS, DIFFERENT OBLIGATIONS

The public relations practitioner works with diverse constituencies. Truthfulness should be the foundation of dealing with everyone. Of course, ways of presenting and disseminating information might vary as audiences vary.

For instance, when in-house public relations professionals target internal audiences—such as fellow employees or corporate shareholders—the mission is principally to inform, while recognizing that the way in which this is done is likely to affect morale and collegiality within the workplace. The rhetoric that might be fitting to cultivate favorable opinion among the general public might not be necessary or appropriate among colleagues.

An example: When Jack in the Box restaurants had to respond to cases of food poisoning caused by serving bad beef, corporate public relations professionals had different publics to target. The mass consumer audience needed to be convinced that the company was taking corrective measures and that overall product quality remained high. Also, corporate employees and franchisees needed reassurance about the integrity of their company's products and management. Similarly, concerns of stockholders in parent company Ralston Purina had to be addressed.

The basic message going to all these publics was fundamentally the same—Jack in the Box expressed its sorrow about the tragic events, had identified the source of the problem (an external meat supplier), was improving quality control, and remained a sound company. As a public relations task, the most effective way to have the desired impact on all the various publics was to present the truth promptly and thoroughly. (These issues are explored at greater length in Chapter Eight.)

In public relations, as in other fields, truth is a precious commodity and should be cherished as such. To take a cavalier approach to the importance of truth is to undermine the integrity and credibility of the profession. For this reason, public relations practitioners should carefully define for themselves the standards of truthfulness to which they will adhere. This is too important a matter for sloppy thinking.

CHAPTER SIX

Working with the News Media

Public relations practitioners and journalists are locked in a symbiotic relationship that is (or should be) governed by intricate professional etiquette based on various ethical principles.

"Etiquette" well describes this relationship's style of governance. It implies formal adherence to established procedure that may sometimes seem unduly rigid. But such formality is preferable to slipping into a casualness that might lead to business catastrophe. Faux pas, especially if committed by the public relations person, can produce embarrassing consequences that could permanently damage a client's interest and disrupt long-term communication with the public through the news media.

For the public relations professional, the ethical imperatives in these matters are rooted in the responsibility to provide the public with accurate information. Because journalists often are indispensable links in the information chain, public relations practitioners must be cognizant of two sets of ethical mandates—their own and those of the news business.

This underscores an important element of ethics theory: Rarely, if ever, do a profession's ethical standards exist in isolation. They must coexist with—and, if possible, truly complement—those of one or more other fields.

UNDERSTANDING EACH OTHER'S ROLES

Before dealing with news organizations, public relations practitioners should possess a good understanding of news-gathering techniques and journalism ethics. Similarly, journalists—who sometimes are curtly dismissive of public relations principles—should remain open-minded as they ponder their public relations counterparts' roles and standards. Particular note should be taken of the differing self-images of the two professions—how each sees its responsibilities to its constituencies.

Journalists (especially reporters and editors engaged in day-to-day news gathering, as opposed to news organizations' corporate executives) see themselves as beholden to no "client" other than the public. In other fields, such as public relations and advertising, communications professionals must split their allegiance between the client, who is paying to get a message delivered to the public, and the public itself, which is relying to some extent on the truthfulness of that message.

Of course, even the reporter on the street knows that his or her news organization has "clients" of a sort—the advertisers who pay most of the costs of gathering and delivering the news. But many news organizations keep a buffer between those who do journalism and those who take care of the business side of the news business.

For instance, if an advertiser objects to being the subject of an accurate, newsworthy story and wants the story changed or withheld, the journalist's job is not to bend to meet the advertiser's demands, but rather to get the news to the public.

Although economic reality sometimes tugs a news organization toward meeting the advertiser's demands, one of the fundamental ethical principles of journalism is to put the public first. This is addressed in the Associated Press Managing Editors code of ethics: "The newspaper should report the news without regard for its own interests. It should not give favored news treatment to advertisers or special-interest groups."[1]

Accuracy is another issue about which journalists' standards may differ from those of public relations professionals. News organizations' product is, ideally, balanced and complete, without spin or other emphasis. The statement of principles of the American Society of Newspaper Editors says, "Every effort must be made to assure that the news content is accurate, free from bias and in context, and that all sides are presented fairly."[2]

In practice, that standard is easier stated than met, as anyone who has felt wronged by a news story will be quick to point out.

Public relations professionals also are committed to accuracy, but the scope of their mandate is defined largely by the interests of their clients. This does not mean that goals of journalism and public relations need be in conflict. Mary Anne Ramer, a journalist-turned-public relations executive, writes: "Journalists worship accuracy in the church of objectivity and the religion of balance. However, much of my PR life has been taken up with persuading reporters to be accurate by being complete in their stories; to be objective by at least considering the other perspective rather than dismissing it as propaganda. . . ."[3]

The commitments to accuracy are similar, if not precisely the same. The journalist's definition is based on responsibility to the reading-viewing-listening audience. As Ramer indicates, the public relations practitioner's perception of accuracy is shaped by dual purposes—to serve the public's need for the truth but at the same time to advance the client's interests.

This kind of mild dissonance contributes to tensions that may arise between the two professions. But professional goals are not (or at least need not be) so diametrically opposed that real enmity must exist. Those who work in each field are trying to do a job, most of them honorably. As long as all parties understand that, peaceful coexistence and even careful cooperation remain possible.

CULTIVATING JOURNALISTS

During the past twenty years, ethics has become increasingly important in the news business. In part, this is a lingering aftereffect of the Watergate scandal, in which investigative reporting played an important part and which culminated in the 1974 resignation of President Richard Nixon. Journalists, engaging in some rare introspection, realized that if their power was such that it could contribute to a president being forced out of office, then that power's use should be guided by thoughtful self-imposed standards. Also, as journalists have intensified their scrutiny of public figures—including the private lives of those public figures—news organizations have realized that they should have their own houses in order before accusing others of wrongdoing. This new emphasis on journalism ethics extends beyond political and investigative reporting and encompasses most of the profession.

Public relations practitioners should take note of this because their relationships with journalists receive expanded ethical scrutiny. The relaxed camaraderie of the past—featuring gift-giving and implicit partnerships—has given way to an ethics-based wariness. The price for not recognizing new sensitivities may be a collapse of communication between a public relations professional and the journalism community.

During the "old days," food and booze were common currency used by public relations professionals to win the hearts and minds of journalists. Holiday seasons, in particular, brought a flood of gifts to ensure goodwill for months to come. Some journalists blame the rise of public relations for a commensurate growth of efforts to seduce journalists into providing favorable coverage. One well-known journalism ethics textbook puts it this way: "As government, business, and other segments of American society came to depend on the advice of professional propagandists and publicists, currying favor with the press soon came to be seen as a necessary or at least helpful step in communicating with the public at large. Currying favor has often translated into gifts, free tickets and trips, free drinks and dinners—the things newspeople call freebies."[4]

News organizations frequently stumbled while trying to control such practices. For instance, one daily newspaper had an unofficial rule that the price of one bottle of Scotch whisky was the outside limit on such gifts. One reporter, however, after seeing a public relations representative deliver large numbers of Scotch bottles to the newsroom, complained to editors. They told him that they could set a stricter rule, but that doing so "might go against the grain of individual reporters who were accustomed to setting their own rules and standards."[5]

More common today are news organizations' guidelines that mirror a provision from the code of ethics of the Society of Professional Journalists: "Gifts, favors, free travel, special treatment or privileges can compromise the integrity of journalists and their employers. Nothing of value should be accepted."[6]

That last sentence has been interpreted in different ways. Does "nothing of value" exclude even a cup of coffee provided at a news conference? Most reporters tend to modify the SPJ standard according to what they consider to be common sense. Presumably, no journalist can be bought for a cup of coffee.

So, a two-part test has evolved:

- Will acceptance of the favor create bias?
- Might the public believe that such bias has been created?

Both questions must be answered "no" before the favor or gift may be accepted.[7]

In practice, individual journalists' standards vary greatly. Some will not accept even the cup of coffee. Others will take virtually anything offered, regardless of value, claiming that no favoritism is being purchased. Some news organizations have their own guidelines about freebies, which they enforce with differing degrees of diligence.

The Public Relations Society of America also addresses these issues in its Code of Professional Standards. Paragraph 6 of the code states (in part), "A member shall not engage in any practice which has the purpose of corrupting the integrity of channels of communications. . . ." This is so vague that it offers little specific guidance, so PRSA offers an official interpretation of the passage.

According to this explanation of paragraph 6's message, public relations professionals should not engage in practices that tend to place a journalist under any obligation to them. Among the prohibited techniques are these:

- giving gifts of more than nominal value
- paying a journalist in exchange for preferential coverage
- hiring a journalist (for example, as a consultant) without the journalist's employer being informed of the relationship
- providing trips unrelated to legitimate news interest
- offering a loan, investment, or advertising to a news organization to obtain preferential coverage

The interpretation further states that paragraph 6 does *not* ban giving meals, entertainment, or trips if news-related. "What is customary or reasonable hospitality," says the interpretation, "has to be a matter of particular judgment in specific situations. In all of these cases, however, it is, or should be, understood that no preferential treatment or guarantees are expected or implied and that complete independence always is left to the media . . . representative."

JUNKET JOURNALISM

One topic causing much controversy is travel. Some news organizations (particularly large and economically healthy ones) have policies against accepting any free travel. Smaller media enterprises and individual free-lance journalists might accept free or discounted trips. The PRSA Code interpretation says: "It is permissible . . . to offer complimentary or discount rates to the media (travel writers, for example) if the rate is for business use and is made available to all writers. Considerable question exists as to the propriety of extending such rates for personal use."

That last sentence speaks to an issue that has generated much debate in journalism and public relations ranks. One notable case features an unlikely villain—Mickey Mouse.

In 1986, Disney World held a fifteenth anniversary party and invited more than ten thousand journalists, other media professionals, and their guests. Underwritten by Disney, hotels, airlines, and state and local visitors' bureaus, the total tab for the three-day event was estimated to be $7.5 million. Invitees were given three options: pay their own way; pay $150 per day to cover part of the costs; or let Disney and the other sponsors pay for all travel, food, and lodging.

Disney World said the offer had "no strings attached" and that the journalists who attended were "not required or expected" to write anything about the event. Disney refused to release names of individuals or news organizations that took advantage of the all-expenses-paid offer, but the company's publicity director said that most of the journalists availing themselves of this option worked for small media companies that might not have been able to participate otherwise.[8]

This "junket journalism" appalled some in the news business. The *New York Times* editorialized that journalists who accepted the free ride from Disney had "debased" their profession and had created the impression that all journalists were "on the take."[9]

Although negative news coverage of this event focused on alleged ethical lapses by journalists, a lesson exists here for public relations professionals. Disney obviously was trying to create goodwill within the press corps, but the company didn't improve its image with those who thought it had instigated unethical behavior by making such an attractive offer. Certainly no journalist was compelled to accept the free trip, but those most irate about this event could make a case that Disney had tried to bribe news organizations and individual journalists. "The Disney trip" is known by many in the news business as an egregious case of slipshod journalistic ethics, and in some quarters Disney is perceived as having been an unscrupulous seducer. Even if blame is placed principally on the journalists, the Disney reputation is tarred by guilt by association.

Despite all the turmoil stirred up by this event, Disney made a similar offer on the occasion of its twentieth anniversary in 1991. This time, controversy centered on NBC's "Today" show. The network accepted free airfare and hotel rooms for thirty "Today" staff members. After this was publicized, NBC decided to reimburse Disney and Delta Airlines, saying it wanted "to avoid even the appearance of conflict or compromise." For its part, Disney denied that it was trying to buy good publicity.[10]

Whatever the intent of those who planned the Disney offerings, the result was to create the impression (at least in some minds) that Disney was being unethically heavy-handed in its efforts to win friends in the news media. Claiming that "we just made the offer, and journalists accepted it" doesn't absolve Disney.

If the Disney executives who engineered this venture had better understood and respected journalism ethics, they might have acted differently. This underscores an important ethical precept: To be ethical in your own profession requires being knowledgeable about the ethics of other professions that you deal with.

Certainly, public relations practitioners should not be expected to back off from providing information that advances their clients' interests. That's a basic part of the job. But it must be done within ethical limits.

In the Disney case, a more appropriate approach would have been to invite newspeople to the anniversary celebrations but not to offer any subsidies. Those journalists who did attend could receive briefings from Disney officials, and be given printed and videotaped information and other creative presentations of the Disney message. Admittedly, the number of journalists participating would be smaller than that in the "free ride" method, but Disney would have accomplished a still-significant public relations task without the negative side effects. Respect can engender goodwill.

The lesson emerging from the Disney case is that, as a general rule, the client's long-term credibility will be strengthened if its public contacts are undertaken ethically.

WORKING RELATIONSHIPS

The bridge between public relations and journalism is information, with the public relations practitioner providing source material on which news stories can be based or supplemented.

That might not seem to be a complicated relationship. One provides and the other receives—pretty simple. But the differing needs and expectations of the two professions bring complexity to this give-and-take.

Many news consumers would be surprised at how much of the journalism they receive originates from public relations sources. For example, while he was managing editor of the *New York Times*, Seymour Topping observed: "Quite a lot of our business stories originate from press releases. It's impossible for us to cover all these organizations ourselves."[11]

A perusal of any newspaper's business section will find evidence of what Topping was talking about. Many of the short items about personnel changes, earnings reports, new product lines, and such are not uncovered by hard-digging investigative reporters. Rather, the information is neatly packaged in a news release and sent to media outlets. Some editors may call for confirmation or further information, but much of the material reaches the public just as a company's public relations representative prepared it.

These short items are newsworthy in a minor way, and most editors will presume the material is accurate. Of course, if the topic is controversial, such as a government investigation of a company or major layoffs, then the news organization's own reporters will develop the story. But even they are likely to call upon the public relations staff for background information and assistance in lining up interviews.

This procedure isn't limited to newspapers' business sections. In the daily flood of information that must be shaped into a journalistic product, public relations also generates much nonbusiness news.

Sometimes, the public relations practitioner does a lot of work that the journalist simply appropriates. One former public relations executive offers this example: "I once spent two months preparing for a new-product announcement by my client. I had to interview product managers, supervise photo sessions, and write fact sheets, speeches and news releases. By the time our news conference was held, there was not much left for reporters to do. They listened to the speeches, asked a few questions, and rewrote my material for publication or broadcast. A few good reporters also talked to other sources about the story. Even then, the job was done in a matter of hours."[12]

In many instances, the format and content of material that public relations practitioners provide to the news media are determined only after sophisticated study. According to Jeff and Marie Blyskal, who are critics of the way the public relations industry influences news coverage, "the smartest PR people do not operate on instinct; they deliberately research the situation and *know* what will sell as news, what will 'package' like news." The goal, say the Blyskals, is to provide material in "such a shape that when the journalist is finished with his or her own hammering, it will still resemble the message the PR people want communicated."[13]

Regardless of the relative proportions of altruism and manipulation, mutual dependence continues. Such cooperation makes everyone's job easier and helps the public get a full picture of whatever is going on. The process moves along unimpeded if—and this is a crucial *if*—the journalists believe that their public relations sources are trustworthy.

For example, John Scanlon—whose clients have included CBS and the law firms representing cigarette manufacturers Philip Morris and Lorillard—is known for his aggressive efforts to influence news coverage. Despite his reputation for abrasiveness, reporters take his calls and listen to what he says. One journalist commented, "In all the times I've dealt with him there's been a lot of froth and hoopla, but when push came to shove, he would tell me the truth, and that's what counts with me."[14]

Reporters know that truth is often a scarce commodity, so they value sources who provide it consistently. Also, journalists are adept at seeing through obfuscation that is just a short step away from being a lie. Here is an example:

REPORTER: "Is your company, XYZ Corporation, thinking about merging with ABC Enterprises?"

XYZ SPOKESPERSON: "At this point in time, we have no plans for a merger. We have no further comment."

This spokesperson's evasion will do nothing more than annoy the reporter. It avoids answering the question about whether a merger may be in the works. It is neither a denial nor a confirmation that a merger might be under consideration. The reporter now will be likely to pursue other sources that may provide information unfavorable to XYZ.

Depending on what XYZ was actually doing, the spokesperson could have said, "We have no interest in merging with ABC Enterprises," or, "We're talking to ABC Enterprises, but nothing has been decided. It would be premature to speculate about what might come of this, but I'll be sure to let you know as soon as we have something solid."

Either of these two answers would probably satisfy—at least temporarily—the reporter. The reason: Each apparently is true. Lying or using "No comment" or other smoke screens might buy a little time, but they won't deter most journalists and won't serve the company's long-term interests.[15] Relying on truth not only is ethical, but also makes good business sense.

Similarly, ethics and common sense should combine to keep puffery within the bounds of reason. For example, suppose a public relations representative is working for a European automobile company that manufactures a compact car selling for $12,000 and widely known to be bare-bones adequate, but nothing more. The public relations person issues a news release that calls it "the finest car on the road, regardless of price." Perhaps someone somewhere thinks that, but basically it's just silly (and untrue). No journalist is going to believe the claim and use it in a news report.

Suppose, however, the release says, "According to Mary Doe, vice president of the American sales division, this car is, in its remarkably low price range, the finest car on the road." Now, the point at least becomes arguable. Reporters probably won't dismiss this claim out of hand. They might even consider the low cost/relative quality issue worth mentioning in a news story.

In ethical terms, the difference between the two statements is one of truthfulness. In practical terms, the difference is that the second claim—the more truthful one—is likely to advance the car company representative's goals. Being ethical pays off.

THE SCREENING PROCESS

Whatever the strategy behind courtship of journalists, public relations practitioners should make some effort to correlate their ethical standards with those of the news business. This isn't a matter of one profession's ethical behavior being better than that of the other. Rather, it simply makes good business sense to avoid possibly alienating those who control an important communications channel.

In the process of getting information to the public, journalists are the gatekeepers, while—in most cases—the public relations professionals are those who must knock on the gate. Journalistic—not public relations—values most often will determine what is allowed through the gate.

A number of studies have found that reporters cite newsworthiness (as opposed to packaging or lobbying) as the primary factor in deciding what information to include in their stories.[16] Newsworthiness is composed of various ingredients. The intrinsic importance of the topic to news consumers is paramount as journalists decide what to print or broadcast, but contributing elements include the reporter's opinion of the veracity of the information.

This is particularly important if the material is delivered by a source (rather than being witnessed or otherwise uncovered firsthand by the reporter), and still more important if the journalist questions the source's motives. As a matter of common journalistic practice, material supplied by public relations sources must pass this more stringent test.

Many journalists are at least skeptical about—if not firmly prejudiced against—public relations practitioners as sources (especially as sole sources). Although attitudes presumably derive from personal experience, some studies suggest that journalists' news judgment is affected by negative predispositions toward public relations sources.[17] Further, although most journalists are not averse to public relations contacts, they often do not perceive the public relations practitioners

with whom they work—or public relations professionals generally—
to be their equals in terms of doing their respective jobs ethically.[18]

Tensions between the two professions reach even into the academic community, where debate continues about the relationship
between journalism and public relations education. Writing about
what he calls the "non-ethical priorities" of public relations, mass
communications Professor Dave Berkman says: "The bottom line in
PR is to make the client look good. If, in a given instance, it happens
that truth and desired image coincide, fine; but that is only a coinci-
dental concern." Offering public relations courses within a journalism program, says Berkman, would mean "bending the ethics behind
journalism."[19]

The notion that public relations practices are intrinsically unethical is simplistic to the point of being just plain wrong. An argument
can easily be made that journalism lends itself to unethical behavior
just as often as public relations does.

But such finger-pointing accomplishes nothing constructive
except to illustrate that bridges between public relations and journalism require constant attention if they are to be kept in good repair.

These tensions can distract members of both professions from
more specific matters that are of greater concern to the public. Principal among these is a facet of the gatekeeper role: deciding whose
stories get told. Journalists shape the issues agenda—what the public
will see and hear—based primarily on what they consider to be newsworthy. Public relations practitioners try to get their clients' concerns
included on that agenda.

Dynamics of the relationship between the two professions should
not obscure the importance of open news channels. The client—be it
General Motors or a community antipoverty program—should have
a fair chance of reaching the public with any newsworthy message.

The ethical task arising in this context is for neither the public
relations practitioner nor the journalist to become so caught up in
interprofessional contentiousness that the duties of representation
and communication are neglected. Both have responsibilities to the
process of conveying information. Goals of the PRSA Code include
better communication, understanding, and cooperation among the
diverse individuals, groups, and institutions of society. These goals
correlate well with journalism's obligation to protect and respond to
the public's right and need to know.

Reaching all those goals requires cooperative as well as autonomous action by public relations and journalism professionals. Such action can emerge only from a relationship rooted in ethical common ground.

CHAPTER SEVEN

Public Relations and the Processes of Government

Since the early days of their profession, public relations practitioners have influenced American politics and government. This is a logical line of work for those whose business is to shape popular sentiment. As Princeton University's Stanley Kelley, Jr., has observed, "Any system of government, autocratic or democratic, owes its life to some kind of support in public opinion."[1]

Practitioners who specialize in politics constitute a specialized cadre within the public relations profession. Some devote themselves exclusively to election campaigns. Others represent issues rather than candidates and concentrate on the legislative process. Still others work within government; democracy is a two-way street, and those who govern must communicate effectively with those who are governed.

In all these areas of concentration, ethical behavior is important. As a constructive force, public relations can be a great asset in a democratic society, aiding the flow of information that links public and government.

But the public relations practitioner should also remember that democratic institutions are fragile, as well as enduring. If, for instance, politicians or those who work for them abuse the process by lying to voters or otherwise campaigning dishonestly, the damage can be great. This will give way to cynicism; participation will yield to apathy. Democracy is sustained by public trust, and all those who work in government and politics have an ethical obligation to respect that trust.

As discussed later in this chapter, the Public Relations Society of America takes special note of these matters in its Code of Professional Standards. Banned are any practices that have "the purpose of corrupting the integrity of . . . the processes of government." Deciding what that means is an ethical test for the public relations practitioner.

ELECTION CAMPAIGNS

Politics offers plenty of opportunity for public relations practitioners skilled in electoral strategies. For instance, campaigners increasingly base their vote-seeking efforts on selling themselves wholesale to mass audiences. In doing so, they rely more heavily on mass communication tools than on traditional political mechanisms such as contacting individual voters and delivering lengthy speeches.

Some public relations professionals who have mastered wholesale politics have gained influence and celebrity. The likes of Democrat James Carville and Republican Ed Rollins sometimes get as much personal news coverage as do the candidates they represent. As a class, political consultants "are permanent; the politicians ephemeral. The consultants have supplanted the old party bosses as the link to the voters."[2]

The job of the public relations practitioner in politics depends on who is defining that job:

- The academic perspective: "Direct the public discourse of important issues, set the agenda in that discussion, and present the candidate as the best possible choice for the public."[3]
- The campaign consultant's view: "Decide what you want the voter to feel or how you want him to react. Decide what you must do to make him react the way you want. Do it."[4]

Ethical issues are particularly important to balance any tendency to overdo this latter approach. Professional responsibility is essential, according to some political observers, since many Americans may become "victims of strategic communication" because they are "easily influenced, easily disillusioned."[5] As practitioners of political public relations become more skilled and as their work becomes more influential in shaping campaign strategies and outcomes, ethical behavior is required if the integrity of the overall political process is to be maintained.

Political public relations is rooted in Edward Bernays's theory about the engineering of consent: "the application of scientific practices and tried practices in the task of getting people to support ideas and programs." "Engineering" connoted a scientific approach, while "consent" reflected Bernays's belief that the public had to be persistently wooed or else it might withdraw its support.[6]

In addition to being a public relations pioneer, Bernays was Sigmund Freud's nephew. Freud, said Bernays, "thought engineering consent was good. . . . He thought it was very American."[7] (Of course, coming from Freud, that wasn't necessarily a compliment. After his only visit to the United States, Freud declared that America was "a gigantic mistake" and was imbued with "unspeakable grimness.")[8]

Bernays also was the first presidential media advisor—professional ancestor of Michael Deaver, David Gergen, and others whose skills are deemed essential if a presidency is to be successful. In an effort to brighten the image of Calvin Coolidge, Bernays arranged for entertainer Al Jolson and some of his vaudeville colleagues to come to the White House for a griddle cake breakfast with the president. Bernays was rewarded with this *New York Times* headline: ACTORS EAT CAKES WITH THE COOLIDGES . . . PRESIDENT NEARLY LAUGHS.[9]

In his work for Coolidge, Bernays was responding to major changes in politics. As one political historian has observed: "Politics once commanded attention as the great American spectator sport; now it had to compete with baseball, vaudeville, and other diversions. Candidates would have to become entertaining, exposing their personalities and adorning their campaigns with the ephemera of modern popular culture," such as celebrity endorsements and feature stories about their family life.[10] This meant, according to *The New Republic* in 1920, that "there is interposed between the voter and his final judgment the whole mechanism of modern publicity."[11]

Such interposition puts the "mechanism of modern publicity"—meaning public relations efforts—in a vital spot in the democratic process and so carries with it special ethical duties. The line between informing and manipulating voters is sometimes hard to discern, but the public relations practitioner should feel obligated to find that line and avoid crossing it.

When the first political public relations firm, Whitaker & Baxter, was launched in California in the 1930s, its stated principles featured a cynicism that raises ethical questions. For instance, one of the firm's precepts was, "The average American doesn't want to be educated; he doesn't want to improve his mind; he doesn't even want to work, consciously, at being a good citizen." Therefore, "put on a show."[12] Journalist Carey McWilliams, watching such principles being put into practice, wrote: "The firm has evolved a style of operation which makes the old-fashioned boss and lobbyists completely obsolete. Whitaker & Baxter has ushered in a new era in American politics— government by public relations."[13]

Many political consultants concern themselves primarily with winning and consign the niceties of democratic responsibility to the second tier of concerns. Joseph Napolitan, a leading consultant to Democratic candidates during the 1960s and '70s, wrote: "I tell people I have no interest in government and don't know anything about it and they think I am joking, but I'm not. My interest is in the political process, the challenge of trying to elect a man to office, with a preference for taking on a candidate who isn't supposed to win and winning with him."[14]

Nothing is intrinsically wrong with being competitive in this way. At issue, however, is perspective—recognizing the nexus between cause and effect. Political game-playing does not take place in a vacuum; it produces officeholders and policies that affect millions of lives. Government is only as good as the politics that creates it. So, trying to divorce political behavior from what it produces is ethically dangerous.

In the midst of a campaign, public relations professionals often shape the public's perception of a candidate. The practitioner is "in a position to know the real abilities, the real aims, the real character of his client. He makes it his profession to know the prejudices, the prejudgments, and the limitations of the public." Because public relations professionals are special pleaders and advocates, they must present their clients in the best possible light and "must flatter the public's estimate of its own competence."[15]

As part of this advocacy, "good public relations agents intentionally set out to thwart the negative aspects of information or images that might be counterproductive to a candidacy or, more important, to build positive images."[16]

Given this influential role, public relations professionals sometimes become relied upon by candidates to shield them from the voters. "Politicians are dependent on the consultants and some pols are strangely fearful when exposed to the public without intermediaries."[17] The farther a candidate is distanced from public scrutiny, the greater the likelihood that voters will receive a postelection surprise. The protective screen that a public relations effort can construct around the superficial aspects of a campaign is unlikely to survive the complex pressures of governing.

Among the public relations functions during a political race is arranging "media events"—those purportedly symbolic moments during which great issues are compressed (and often trivialized) so they will fit into ten seconds of video. In the tradition of one pretelevision media event, the Boston Tea Party, ambience has become as important as substance. For example, during the 1988 presidential campaign, when Republican strategists decided that the issue of the day was "patriotism," they arranged an event for George Bush at a flag factory, so he could be seen awash in a sea of red, white, and blue.

That may seem extreme, but few limits confine the tastelessness that is part of many campaigns. Another case from 1988: Albert Gore, then a presidential candidate, was demonstrating his concern about health care by touring a neonatal intensive care unit at a New York hospital. Amidst sick babies and medical hardware, reporters and photographers record the words and actions of the candidate. Ideally, from the campaign consultant's standpoint, this event will produce an image of a sensitive Gore, a man who would be a compassionate president. But as one member of that day's press entourage wrote: "We stand there all thinking the same thing: What the hell are we doing here? Why is this necessary? And when will either the press or the candidates develop some sense of shame?"[18] Those questions are worth pondering by the public relations professionals who arrange such events.

It should go without saying that being truthful is an ethical responsibility. But in politics, "truth" sometimes gets stretched into outlandish shapes. Particularly as election day draws closer, temptations increase to go beyond even the most generous boundaries of truth.

Consider this case: On November 2, 1992—the day before the election—the National Republican Campaign Committee issued a news release that said in part: "There have been persistent rumors in Washington that Bill Clinton is having an affair with a member of the traveling press that has been covering him on this presidential campaign. . . . It is incumbent on the nation's media to find out if it is true. If it is not true, it ought to be exposed as the rumor that it is."[19]

Those who issued this release and faxed it to news organizations throughout the country had one goal—to stimulate a last-minute burst of negative news stories about Clinton's character and to derail his anticipated victory.

With no evidence and no witnesses except anonymous sources, journalists did not report the story. Merely reporting a rumor gives it the imprimatur of truth. For the news media, *not* reporting this rumor was the ethical thing to do.

But what about the public relations side of this matter? Certainly, plenty of rumors had been floating around, both before and after the Gennifer Flowers scandal had erupted in first the tabloid and then the mainstream media. As an advocate for the Republican campaign, is it appropriate for a public relations professional to provide the press with an unsubstantiated story and hope for useful results? After all—the reasoning might go—news organizations will decide for themselves what, if anything, gets to the public. So what is unethical about providing an initial push that might or might not result in news stories?

Article 6 of the PRSA Code of Professional Standards says, "A member shall not engage in any practice which has the purpose of corrupting the integrity of channels of communications or the processes of government." At issue in the Clinton case was dissemination of unsubstantiated information (which was probably known to be untrue by those who were supplying it). It might have affected an election outcome and so may well have constituted "corrupting the integrity of channels of communication" in the electoral part of the "processes of government." Claiming that "we just gave it to the news media and they decided how to use it" does not absolve the source from responsibility.

The fast pace of campaigning in this era of satellites and fax machines means that ethical judgments must be made quickly and constantly. According to one political journalist: "The immediacy of

TV and radio has forced political strategists to alter their methods to keep up. The development and dissemination of political messages, at least in major races, has turned into a form of high-tech jai alai, where messages hurled at the speed of light have to be responded to immediately." A campaign consultant offers an adage about how this works: "It's hard for the other guy to say dirty things about you if your fist is in his mouth."[20]

For public relations professionals who work in campaigns, ethical responsibility should transcend—or, perhaps more realistically, accompany—concerns about who wins and loses the election. Loyalty to process should match loyalty to client.

LOBBYING

Speaking to reporters in 1913, President Woodrow Wilson said that Washington was so full of lobbyists that "a brick couldn't be thrown without hitting one." In the battle raging about a tariff bill, warned the President, "It is of serious interest to the country that the people at large should have no lobby and be voiceless in these matters, while great bodies of astute men seek to create an artificial opinion and to overcome the interests of the public for their private profit."[21]

This was by no means the first excoriation of lobbying; James Madison had criticized such "mischiefs of faction" in the Federalist Papers. But as Woodrow Wilson and everyone else who has worked in government quickly learned, the public's business is always susceptible to pressure from private interests.

In 1933, a presidential commission reported that lobbying was changing. Instead of direct contact and campaign contributions from those who were personally involved in an issue, lobbying was being conducted by "professional press agents, public relations counsels and propagandists."[22]

Lobbying is one of the most controversial activities of the public relations profession. Depending on who is defining it, lobbying is crass, barely legal manipulation of the political process, or it is an enhancement of democracy that gives citizens better access to their government.

The former definition has plenty of evidence to support it. In one recent case involving a proposed minor change to Medicare regulations, members of Congress received letters from elderly constituents with a common message: "If the change is enacted, my husband will die," or some slight variation thereon. The letters were almost the same, word for word. As it happened, the writers' fears were not grounded in fact; the proposed change would have no such effect. The invisible lobbyists behind this letter-writing effort had been untruthful and manipulative.[23]

On the other hand, lobbying sometimes is open and constructive. In the aftermath of Hurricane Andrew's destruction in 1992, the Department of Housing and Urban Development wanted to revise safety guidelines for mobile homes. The American Society of Civil Engineers backed a public relations campaign to support new standards. A spokesman for the engineers said people who live in mobile homes have a right to be safe, adding that when unsafe homes are destroyed, "our members are the ones who have to clean the stuff up."[24] (Worth noting is the counterlobbying effort launched by the Manufactured Housing Institute, which claimed that the engineers' standards would push construction costs too high.)

The number of lobbyists remains something of a mystery. Loopholes in federal laws have let many lobbyists avoid registering. (The Justice Department in 1983 called the Federal Regulation of Lobbying Act of 1946 unenforceable.) An educated estimate of the number of lobbyists in Washington is fifteen thousand, with many more scattered throughout the country.[25]

Even those who make their living this way know that they are held in low regard by much of the public. Longtime lobbyist Jerry Jasinowski of the National Association of Manufacturers says people think "we are a small group, in Gucci shoes, somehow controlling issues in a way that is at variance with the public interest."[26] And one journalist writes: "In the abstract, lobbying kindles an image of wickedness only barely less disreputable than the skullduggery of the Mafia. . . . It has the illicit aroma of cigar smoke, booze, and money delivered in brown envelopes."[27]

In his book *Power in Washington*, Douglass Cater details the work of one lobbyist, Samuel Stavisky, a former *Washington Post* reporter who described himself as a "management consultant in public relations and government relations." According to Cater: "He managed to focus the attention of distracted policy-makers on his problem, to trigger actions by some, and to thwart actions by others. Probably none of the policy-makers did anything that he did not wish to do, but a good many might have been too preoccupied or too timid to do what they did if they had not been egged on."[28]

That does not sound too bad in itself, but the tactics used by Stavisky (who represented sugar manufacturers in pre-Castro Cuba) merit scrutiny. One of his strategies was to get news stories published that were favorable to his clients. So, he took journalists to dinner at Washington's finest restaurants and made his case. He picked up the tab. He encouraged reporters to go to Cuba and gave travel subsidies to those whose publications wouldn't finance them. He even covered the gambling losses that one reporter incurred in Havana.[29]

All this was going on during the 1950s, when ethical standards were considerably more lax than they are now. But this kind of lobbying is far from obsolete today, even if it is less visible. In addition to the journalists' behavior in the Stavisky case violating most news organizations' codes of ethics, such tactics by a public relations practitioner would run afoul of the PRSA Code of Professional Standards.

The PRSA's official interpretation of code article 6 (about "corrupting the integrity of channels of communications") addresses these matters. For instance, the code prohibits practices that place media representatives "under any obligation to the member." Specifically, this includes "giving of gifts of more than nominal value" and "any form of payment or compensation to a member of the media in order to obtain preferential or guaranteed news or editorial coverage." Also, the code limits subsidized travel to occasions when it "is made available to all writers." The Stavisky trips and his covering a reporter's gambling debt probably fall outside the code's definition of ethical practice.

Unethical behavior by public relations practitioners who engage in lobbying not only gives the profession a bad name, it also can get the practitioner into serious legal trouble. Michael Deaver—a long-time top aide to President Ronald Reagan—left the White House in 1986 and immediately opened a public and governmental relations office. His clients included major corporations and foreign governments. He was the subject of a *Time* magazine cover story and bragged, "There's no question I've got as good access as anybody." He used that access, however, to lobby government officials within a year after leaving the president's staff and worked on issues that he had been involved with while a government employee. That is against the law.

For example, as a White House aide, Deaver had participated in meetings about problems with Canada concerning acid rain. As soon as he began his private business, he received a $105,000 lobbying contract from the Canadians. After telling a federal grand jury that he did not remember several of the specific contacts of which he was accused, he was indicted for—and later convicted of—perjury.[30]

This was a classic case of the worst kind of influence peddling. Besides being illegal, Deaver's behavior appears to have been in direct contravention of the PRSA Code standard about corrupting the integrity of the processes of government.

Not all lobbying is a matter of making fat cats fatter. Many public relations practitioners earn credit for themselves and their profession by enhancing the voices of those who might otherwise go unheard in the rush of governance. For example, when families of persons with Alzheimer's disease want to make a case for more federally supported research, public relations professionals can help them lobby Congress in several ways, such as arranging direct contact with members and staff and stimulating public support for the cause by increasing awareness about the issue.

In this way, public relations enhances democracy, helping to make sure that disparate interests receive attention from the public and policymakers. Public relations counsel can serve as an equalizer, using ingenuity and persistence to pull the spotlight beams of news media and government toward individuals, organizations, and causes that deserve attention but might lack the clout and expertise to get it on their own.

That is the good side—honest representation. Unfortunately, the same skills used in ethical lobbying can be turned to unethical purposes. Deception and manipulation happen often enough to be a major ethical concern for the public relations profession.

The following case illustrates the ease with which ethical boundaries may be crossed. It involves one of the best-known public relations firms—Hill and Knowlton—and one of the most important events in recent years—the Persian Gulf War.

Shortly after Iraq occupied Kuwait in 1990, Hill and Knowlton was hired by Citizens for a Free Kuwait (CFK), an organization funded by Kuwaitis interested in rallying American public opinion behind the cause of liberating Kuwait. With at least $6 million put at its disposal by CFK, Hill and Knowlton embarked on a comprehensive campaign to make Americans willing to do whatever was necessary to eject the Iraqis from Kuwait.

The most controversial tactic employed by Hill and Knowlton was to publicize a claim that Iraqi soldiers had come into Kuwaiti hospitals, stolen pediatric incubators, and left the babies who had been in them on the floor to die. Dramatic presentation of this charge was made by a witness at a congressional caucus meeting, a fifteen-year-old who identified herself only by her first name, Nayirah. Her story about "incubator atrocities" was cited by President George Bush six times in a month. It was a significant factor in the concerted campaign to fortify Americans' resolve to go to war to liberate Kuwait.

The quick defeat of Saddam Hussein's forces in the Desert Storm offensive of early 1991 achieved the goal of Citizens for a Free Kuwait. Hill and Knowlton had been successful.

Not until the following year did most Americans learn that Nayirah is not just any Kuwaiti. She is the daughter of Kuwait's ambassador to the United States and a member of that country's royal family. Investigative stories by ABC News reporter John Martin and other journalists found no corroboration of the incubator story. In fact, doctors who had worked at the hospital where Nayirah had been a volunteer told reporters that the incident simply did not happen. Also, it was learned that of the $12 million collected by Citizens for a Free Kuwait—supposedly an organization of concerned individuals acting privately—$11.8 million came from the Kuwaiti government.[31]

The hearing at which Nayirah testified was held by the Human Rights Caucus, which lacks the legal status of a true congressional committee. As one journalist observed, "Lying under oath in front of a congressional committee is a crime; lying under the cover of anonymity to a caucus is merely public relations."[32]

From all this, questions arise: Did Hill and Knowlton go too far when it acted on results from focus groups to determine that atrocity stories would be most effective in making Americans more likely to support U.S. military action? Was the firm deceptive when it did not disclose the fact that the star witness at the congressional hearing was the Kuwaiti ambassador's daughter, a fact that certainly would have generated some skepticism about her testimony?

Hill and Knowlton says "no" to such questions. In a *New York Times* letter to the editor, Thomas Eidson, the firm's president and chief executive officer, said, "At no time has this firm collaborated with anyone to produce knowingly deceptive testimony."[33] Eidson also defended the complex financial relationship that existed between Hill and Knowlton and the Congressional Human Rights Foundation, which had close ties to the congressional caucus before which Nayirah testified.

Fixing blame in this complicated case is less important than is recognizing how easy it is to slip from straightforward representation into deception and manipulation. Hill and Knowlton was hired to influence opinion. It did so by drafting a speech and press packet materials, setting up news conferences, prepping pro-Kuwait sources for interviews, organizing Kuwait Information Day on college campuses and a national day of prayer for Kuwait in churches, and even ordering "Free Kuwait" T-shirts.[34] All that is standard practice. But the failure to reveal Nayirah's true identity and the extent of the Kuwaiti government's involvement in efforts to push America toward war raises questions about the firm's ethics.

Also among the Hill and Knowlton attention-getters were photographs that purportedly documented Iraqi atrocities. At first glance, some of the pictures displayed by Citizens for a Free Kuwait were particularly horrific, apparently of Kuwaitis who had been tortured and murdered. But careful scrutiny of the slightly out-of-focus photos revealed that the "people" depicted were actually mannequins. Supposedly, the depictions were based on real executions, but this was only vaguely documented.[35]

The Hill and Knowlton campaign certainly helped its clients. The baby incubators story, for instance, became one of the most frequently cited justifications for taking harsh action against Iraq. By the time Desert Storm was over and the emir of Kuwait had returned, Hill and Knowlton was no longer working for Citizens for a Free Kuwait. But one Hill and Knowlton executive, noting the publicity about torture and execution of alleged collaborators by the reinstated Kuwaiti government, said, "That's when they really needed the PR."[36]

Sophisticated strategies such as were employed in this case have led to increasingly critical scrutiny of the ethics of lobbying and those who do it. Although Hill and Knowlton was able to claim great success for its client's cause, the firm's reputation suffered. Lobbying per se has no established ethical guidelines (although aspects of it are governed by law), but when public relations practitioners engage in lobbying, the ethical standards of their own profession should be observed.

The art of lobbying continues to evolve. Members of a new breed of lobbyists earn their fees based on what they know, rather than whom they know; the emphasis is on process more than personalities. As one lobbyist puts it: "Information is the currency of Capitol Hill, not dollars. And not friends."[37] Also, more importance is accorded to orchestrating grass roots pressure—using public relations techniques to stimulate public political action such as letter-writing campaigns. Worth noting is that such grass roots lobbying usually is outside the scope of disclosure requirements contained in recent lobbying regulations.[38] Legal as well as ethical loopholes are plentiful.

REPRESENTING THE GOVERNMENT

The explosive growth of government is a topic that politicians love to moan about, even while they contribute to it. Regardless of what may be right and wrong about this expansion, sheer size often makes more tenuous the links between government and people. Particularly as functions of government shift from highly visible bodies such as the Congress to less frequently scrutinized bureaucratic offices, the strands of communication essential to a democratic system become stretched and frayed. Making sure the governed know what the governors are doing is a public relations task. So, too, is ensuring that the officials and agencies of government know what each other is doing.

Despite the integral role of public relations in a democracy, practitioners of governmental public relations often face more hostility than their nongovernmental colleagues do. Among the factors contributing to this are tensions between government and the news media, between the executive and legislative branches, between the major political parties, and between the government and private interests with a large stake in regulatory and other government actions.[39] All these conflicts limit trust and encourage skepticism. That makes public relations more important and more difficult.

Further complicating governmental public relations work is a widespread public perception that much of the information coming from the government is self-serving propaganda. Not only do many citizens not trust what the government says, they often become incensed when they learn about expensive dissemination of the government's side of issues. The equating of public relations and propagandizing has led some governmental bodies to take refuge behind semantics, using "press secretary" or "public information specialist" as the official title for a public relations practitioner. Feeling the heat, Congress once passed a law banning the spending of any part of an appropriation on "publicity experts" unless specifically approved by Congress.[40]

That was in 1913. Since then, public relations has become an integral function within most of government. By the late 1980s, public relations personnel in the federal government reached an estimated total of thirteen thousand, consuming about $2.5 billion in tax money each year.[41] Virtually every part of government has its own public relations contingent. For instance, as the Vietnam War drew to a close in the mid-1970s, the U.S. armed forces employed approximately three thousand people in public relations tasks, spending more than $50 million annually.[42]

A particularly ingenious example of executive branch public relations was the "Journalist in Space" program launched by the National Aeronautics and Space Administration (NASA). Journalists were invited to compete for a spot on a space shuttle crew by undergoing a process much like applying to college (including writing an essay about why they should be chosen). While this selection process was under way, many of these prospective journalist-astronauts were likely to be well disposed toward NASA and were not likely to risk their chances by writing negative stories. This project was cut short by the explosion of the *Challenger*, but the venture remains a classic case of using a gimmick to influence public opinion.

Public relations specialists working for government agencies must appeal to diverse publics:

- Within their own agency or branch, they keep partners in complex working relationships informed about what each other is doing. For example, the Department of Housing and Urban Development and the Department of Health and Human Services may be offering complementary programs to residents of public housing projects. To avoid duplication of effort and ensure most effective delivery of services, personnel in the two departments need to be well informed about their counterparts' activities. This is an internal communications task (and therefore a facet of public relations).

- Within the larger governmental context, they inform other branches about their activities, as when an agency publicizes its work prior to a congressional appropriations vote. As government has grown larger, the need—particularly for executive branch agencies—to establish clear identities has become essential if the agencies' funding is to be maintained. For instance, the Department of Agriculture might make certain before its budget is voted on that each member of Congress is well informed about the department's activities in his or her district.
- Related to both these functions, they provide information to the public. Besides the responsibility of government to let its constituents know what it is doing, public support is essential as a political matter.

    For instance, a congressional committee charged with oversight of an agency is much more likely to be favorably disposed toward that agency if the committee members believe that their constituents are well informed about that agency's work. A highly visible example can be seen in the public relations work conducted by the Department of Defense (and its subsidiary departments, such as the Department of the Navy). The often-stormy relationship between the Pentagon and Capitol Hill inspires many Defense Department efforts to win public support.

Some examples:

- The Blue Angels aerial show travels the country partly as a recruiting tool, but also as a way to spark public enthusiasm for military aviation programs and support for funding those programs.
- During the Cold War, military intelligence information was often used as a basis for public relations efforts designed to justify spending programs.

    On the other hand, scandals such as the Navy Tailhook affair—in which Navy pilots and high-ranking officers were accused of sexual misconduct—require public relations as damage control.

The principal ethical question arising in all these cases is: To whom is principal loyalty owed—the public or the client (in this case, the government)? To what extent, for example, should the benefits of a proposed government program be appraised with one-sided optimism? At what point does that rose-colored view—which is designed to win intragovernmental and public support—become unethical exaggeration?

Probably the best-known source of governmental public relations efforts is the White House. Rarely does a day go by that doesn't include an event or news release designed to influence public opinion. Watch a president in action for a few hours: a Rose Garden bill-signing, a photo session with some Olympic athletes, an Oval Office meeting with congressional leaders. Each of these has its carefully planned public relations purpose, ranging from presenting the president as active, thoughtful, compassionate, or whatever other quality seems most important at the moment to those in charge of shaping and maintaining his image.

White House public relations efforts often are closely linked to polling data. For instance, when polls showed that Americans opposed by a two-to-one margin President Reagan's proposed cutbacks in federal spending on education, White House public relations boss Michael Deaver orchestrated nationwide dissemination of speeches and other information about merit pay for teachers, smaller class sizes, and other ideas the president endorsed. This worked; new polling showed that opinion had turned around, registering two-to-one *in favor* of Reagan's policies.[43]

Presidential public relations efforts should not be viewed as just manipulative political ploys. Effective governing requires effective public relations. For example, when a president visits a community that has suffered great damage from flood, earthquake, or other disaster, cynics might say that he is only doing so to spruce up his image. That may be part of it, but he is also talking with his constituents and seeing things that will affect how he directs the federal response to the crisis. And he is letting people know that their president cares about their plight. All this is good public relations, but it also is good governance.

The intricacies of political and governmental public relations underscore the importance of *motive* as an ethical factor. Sometimes, a public relations effort is undertaken solely to manipulate people's emotions and attitudes in order to benefit its sponsor's self-interest. That probably goes beyond ethically acceptable practice, violating standards such as the PRSA ban on corrupting the integrity of processes of government.

In most cases, however, the desire of politicians to bolster their images is merely a part of their larger desire to serve the public. As the natural disaster ploy illustrates, a good motive—and even a mixed motive—brings the public relations project within ethical bounds.

SELF-POLICING IN POLITICAL PUBLIC RELATIONS

Michael Deaver's ethical and legal transgressions called attention to the difficulties sometimes faced by public relations professionals who work in both the public and private sectors. This issue attracted news media attention again during the early stages of Bill Clinton's presidency. The top public relations specialists from his 1992 campaign decided not to take jobs within the administration, but rather to remain on the private side, where they could make more money and handle diverse clients. Nevertheless, these four people—James Carville, Paul Begala, Mandy Grunwald, and Stanley Greenberg— were issued special security passes allowing easy entry to the White House. And many of the projects they worked on were for the president's benefit.

Members of this Clinton team went to work for the Democratic National Committee, political candidates, and causes such as the North American Free Trade Agreement (NAFTA). As reported in *Business Week*, this raises ethical questions: "Never before have so many key political advisers plied their trade as free-lancers—freed from the restrictive conflict-of-interest rules that govern Administration appointees. This dual role worries government watchdog groups. The four 'are operating in an ethical netherworld,' contends Ellen S. Miller, director of the Center for Responsive Politics. 'The fact that they have a close relationship with the White House while maintaining outside clients raises the specter of conflict of interest.'"[44]

Grunwald reported that when the four—who often work independently of each other—found that few legal restrictions applied to their work, they established their own ethical guidelines, including a self-imposed ban on corporate lobbying and representing foreign governments. Nevertheless, their prospective clients are likely to believe that by hiring one of these consultants they will be buying influence. The *appearance* of using White House ties to boost business lingers. Public perception of professional practices should be of concern to practitioners who want to be considered ethical.

This is clearly a rough-and-tumble kind of work. Because political public relations is imbued with so many ethical challenges, the PRSA offers an official interpretation of its code as it applies to this field. The definition of "political public relations" encompasses managing campaigns, counseling officeholders or government bodies, lobbying, and other tasks. In its eleven clauses, the PRSA interpretation prohibits a practitioner from preparing or disseminating false, misleading, or unattributed campaign material, or from trying to buy influence with gifts or other contributions. It requires PRSA members to be conversant with the complex array of campaign laws. It also underscores the importance of disclosing potential conflicts of interest and respecting the confidentiality of clients' information.

By devoting a lengthy special interpretation of its code to political public relations, the PRSA acknowledges the number and complexity of ethical challenges likely to arise in political work. The implicit message to practitioners is "Be extra careful."

LITIGATION SUPPORT

The legal system is another field of government in which the role of public relations has expanded. Recognizing the indirect impact of public opinion on outcomes in the civil and criminal justice processes, lawyers and other advocates for issues before the courts have turned to public relations practitioners for help. Plenty of controversy has resulted.

A 1993 *New York Times* column stated that "litigation blackmail is being committed in the U.S. every day, aided and abetted by journalists, lawyers and public relations professionals." According to the writer, the integrity of the legal process is being seriously undermined by lawsuits being tried in the court of public opinion, rather than in the court of law. "It is not the function of the press, or of those who disseminate news and information on the fringes of journalism—like talk shows—to allow the merits of individual cases to be argued or promoted outside due process."[45]

Although such criticism arguably should be directed at members of the media who are ultimately responsible for deciding what information about judicial proceedings will be made public, the role of public relations in this process can be significant. Because public relations has become an influential factor in trial publicity, the ethics of its use warrants examination.

Recognizing the impact of public opinion on both the party's reputation and potentially on the outcome of the case, more and more parties to civil lawsuits and criminal cases (and their attorneys) are turning to public relations counselors for help. These parties have two objectives: to maintain their credibility with the public and to influence the decision makers involved in the case.

The role of public relations in maintaining a client company's reputation during litigation seldom raises questions of impropriety; in fact, this is simply good crisis management. For example, when American Airlines was involved in a federal antitrust lawsuit in which the company was charged with trying to run two weaker carriers out of business, legal and public relations counselors were kept busy.

American's top public relations officer, Tim Doke, explained: "If we allow the imagery that the attorneys and the spokesmen for our competitors have laid out for the news media to absorb and to linger, we would be paying many kinds of costs in correcting that damage in the perception of the general public. . . . [The public] could be dramatically affected by the messages that come out of the trial."[46]

Essentially, the company was trying to level the playing field by making its side known to a public that had been exposed to negative accusations regarding the company's business practices. Few would challenge the company's right to defend itself against such charges. This is simply part of being considered innocent until proven guilty.

It is the second objective—to influence the outcome of the case— that has been criticized as being unethical and in violation of the PRSA Code requirement that members avoid corrupting "channels of communications and processes of government." Critics charge that practitioners who participate in litigation are interfering with due process and damaging the integrity of the judicial system.

Others disagree. According to public relations executive John Saffir, public relations has become an effective, influential component of legal maneuvering. "Like it or not, public relations is a considerable factor today, in building reputations, marketing products, influencing stockholders—and in conducting lawsuits."

In response to critics, Saffir says it is not that the judge or jury will be so influenced by stories planted in the media that they will give one side a break. Rather, he says that what appears in print and on television helps to shape the environment of opinion within which attitudes are adopted and judgments are formed.

"Juries do not deliberate in a vacuum. Their memories are not wiped clean when they enter the jury box. Even judges have been known to read the papers and watch TV. So if you can skew the perception of jurors and judges in your favor, your chances of a favorable outcome are enhanced. Your legal counsel handles legal matters and courtroom advocacy. Your public relations counsel engineers the perceptions of those who will decide your case."[47]

This "engineering of perceptions" does not proceed unchecked in the courtroom. For example, during jury selection, the judge and attorneys for all parties will be appraising the potential jurors' preconceptions about the case, however they may have been created. Some of these prospective jurors might not have seen or heard the case-related public relations efforts, and even those who were exposed may not have had their objectivity affected. Ultimately, it is the trial court's responsibility to detect potential prejudice and ensure participants a fair trial.

Practitioners involved in what has come to be called "litigation public relations" must be extremely careful to focus on presenting facts rather than trying to manipulate minds in ways that might interfere with judicial process. The public relations professional's obligation is to ensure that his or her client receives a fair trial in the court of public opinion. Ensuring that all parties are treated fairly in the court of law should be left to the legal professionals.

Whenever and however public relations professionals are involved in the processes of government, they assume ethical responsibilities commensurate with the importance of safeguarding democratic institutions. In a free society, those institutions are particularly susceptible to abuse. That is why the individual public relations professional must take seriously his or her work in this field, and why the profession collectively must police itself thoughtfully and rigorously.

CHAPTER EIGHT

Ethical Challenges in Crisis Public Relations

The greatest tests of public relations ethics are likely to arise during times of crisis. The stakes are high, the pressure is great, and the allure of expedience is hard to resist. The ethical decision-making process is accelerated. As far as many clients and employers are concerned, this is when public relations practitioners earn their keep.

Crises help define the moral purpose of public relations. More than just a matter of process, crisis public relations is an ethical testing ground. These occasions test an important maxim: Ethical public relations is good public relations.

In many such instances, public relations professionals are the vital links in a chain that delivers information that the public wants and needs to know. The two principal cases discussed in this chapter make clear that public relations professionals have dual responsibilities to client and public. The practitioners' work on these occasions had direct impact on the levels of panic and anger that were generated by the crisis events.

Ethical public relations professionals approach crisis work with particular concern for the systemic ramifications of their efforts. They can do much good or cause much damage.

TYLENOL

On September 30, 1982, Johnson & Johnson announced that three persons had died as a result of taking Tylenol capsules that had been laced with cyanide. Within the next two days, four additional deaths from the same cause were reported. All seven deaths occurred in the

Chicago area, but Johnson & Johnson recalled thirty-one million bottles of Tylenol from store shelves throughout the nation. (The Tylenol had been produced by McNeil Consumer Products, a Johnson & Johnson subsidiary.)

The publicity surrounding this incident was unprecedented in American business history; in the print media alone, more than 125,000 stories appeared.[1] Many business analysts said that no product could survive this, and they pronounced Tylenol dead as a product line.

Tylenol was not just any merchandise. During the 1970s, Tylenol had become the biggest-selling item in drug, food, and mass-merchandising outlets (ending the eighteen-year dominance of Procter & Gamble's Crest toothpaste). With annual sales totaling $1.2 billion, Tylenol products controlled 37 percent of the over-the-counter analgesics market.[2] After the poisonings, that share dropped to 7 percent.

But in what some business experts called the greatest comeback since Lazarus, Tylenol rebounded within just six months to reclaim 30 percent of the market.

The poisoners had not been caught. The drug itself had not changed. And yet public confidence in the brand was restored. This was a triumph of public relations, a classic example of the effectiveness of well-managed grace under pressure.

From the outset of the crisis, Johnson & Johnson recognized the immediate and long-term stakes involved. Its strategy was based on maintaining high visibility and avoiding any appearance that the corporation was trying to duck responsibility. This held true even when it was quickly determined that the bottles almost certainly were laced in retail stores rather than in the company's manufacturing or distribution process.

Johnson & Johnson chairman James Burke spearheaded an effort to win public trust. It included the following immediate and long-term measures:

- In addition to ordering the recall, Burke was consistently available to the media, holding news conferences and appearing on programs such as "60 Minutes" and "Donahue." Also, reporters were provided with video excerpts of briefings conducted by corporate officers and footage showing Tylenol's manufacturing process.

- The corporation's closed-circuit news channel was used to provide employees with news conference excerpts and other updates. Versions of this video about the company's response were sent to wholesalers and retailers.[3]
- A pep rally was held for the company's 2,250 sales representatives, at which they were told that their company was recovering. They were urged to make the case for Tylenol to physicians and pharmacists.
- An 800 telephone number was established so that consumers could ask company officials about the poisonings or the product.
- Corporate officials remained visibly committed to the law enforcement investigation of the murders, offering more than $100,000 in reward money.
- Within ten weeks, the company reintroduced Tylenol to the market, putting the product back on store shelves in new, triple-sealed packages.
- The company marketed the "new" Tylenol aggressively, using tactics such as giving away eighty million coupons good for $2.50 toward purchase of any Tylenol product, and launching a soft-sell advertising campaign that featured testimonials about consumer trust in Tylenol.

Collectively, these measures illustrate smart and ethical public relations strategy. By making himself a "media personality," at least temporarily, Burke transformed Johnson & Johnson from corporation to person in the public's eyes. Also, by meeting with reporters and appearing on talk shows, Burke was backing up Johnson & Johnson's claim that it had nothing to hide. Forthright dealing with the public is sound ethics and good business.

Also, reaching out to employees is an example of a public relations effort targeted at an in-house public. A closed-circuit television network is an effective way to keep the entire corporate family aware of what is going on, and a pep rally approach can improve morale and foster unity. Part of the corporate public relations function is to recognize and respond to the needs of diverse publics. Along these lines, employees, as well as consumers, merit ethical treatment.

Harold Burson, chairman of Burson-Marsteller Public Relations and a consultant to Johnson & Johnson, later wrote, "By taking the offensive and addressing the concerns, real and imagined, of key audiences, a company is more likely to be viewed as a responsible and responsive citizen rather than a recalcitrant or indifferent monolith."[4]

Johnson & Johnson's effective defining of its own image in the midst of crisis attracted many admiring comments. One Wall Street observer said: "Johnson & Johnson management were quick to cast themselves in the role of self-sacrificing servants of the people. They generated enormous public sympathy and managed to convince most Tylenol consumers that [the consumers] owed the company cooperation in saving the product."[5]

All this worked, and the process that Johnson & Johnson relied on in 1982 proved a valuable precedent when another Tylenol poisoning crisis occurred in 1986.

A woman in a New York City suburb died of cyanide poisoning after taking two Tylenol capsules. Several days later, more cyanide-laced capsules were found in a store nearby. Once again, the company pulled all its Tylenol capsules off store shelves throughout the country. And once again, chairman James Burke appeared on network newscasts, expressing sympathy for the victim's family and urging consumers to try the new Tylenol caplets—solid pills that replaced the gel-covered (and presumably easier-to-contaminate) capsules.

This time the public relations strategy had an extra twist. In addition to reassuring consumers about Tylenol generally, Johnson & Johnson needed to convince these consumers to stick with the brand while abandoning popular, easy-to-swallow capsules. Although Burke denied it, some market analysts said that the public relations effort was designed in part to make this crisis more about capsules than about Tylenol and thus force competitors—such as the makers of Excedrin and Anacin—also to drop their popular capsule products.[6]

For the most part, however, Burke's motives were not challenged. His high visibility contributed to his becoming something of a folk hero. He later agreed that his television appearances had been effective. "The public," he said, "knows if you're being straight with them, and they usually sense it if you aren't. That's one of the things about television. It has a tendency to reveal us as we really are."[7] This underscores a practical reason for being ethical: If you're not, you're more likely to be found out because of the television camera's intense scrutiny.

Even President Ronald Reagan joined in the praise of Burke, telling him at a White House ceremony, "In recent days you have lived up to the very highest ideals of corporate responsibility."[8] And *Business Week* editorialized: "Business takes a lot of lumps these days—sometimes with good reason—so when a company emerges from a crisis like this one with credit to itself, it deserves notice. . . . Burke acted promptly to protect the public, at great cost to his company. By doing so, he has shown a keen sense for good public relations—and, more important, for public responsibility."[9]

That linkage of public relations and public responsibility is the essence of ethical behavior in this field. Johnson & Johnson's forthright response in the Tylenol crises also showed that good ethics is good business.

But not all corporations follow Johnson & Johnson's lead. Sometimes the alternative—a "hunker down and let it all blow over" approach—may work. But often, especially if the magnitude of the crisis at hand is great enough, the public has little patience for what it considers to be unethical behavior, such as stonewalling.

The next case illustrates how a flawed public relations strategy can contribute to substantial, lasting damage that a corporation may incur during a crisis.

EXXON VALDEZ

On March 24, 1989, the tanker Exxon Valdez tore itself open on a reef in Alaska's Prince William Sound and spilled more than ten million gallons of crude oil. The resulting environmental chaos attracted massive international media coverage that often portrayed Exxon Corporation as the villain.

Exxon's problems were exacerbated by its apparent lack of preparation and its hesitancy in dealing with the news media. CEO Lawrence Rawl stayed out of public view for nearly a week after the Valdez ran aground.

This low-profile approach to a high-profile crisis served only to antagonize the public. Exxon quickly came to be seen by many as a greedy, insensitive despoiler of the environment. Symbolic boycotts were organized, and some politicians and media commentators urged consumers to cut up their Exxon credit cards. (Exxon reported that by a month after the Valdez incident, it had received six thousand cut-up cards, out of seven million that were in use.) Environmental groups took advantage of Exxon's defensiveness to push the case for limiting further oil operations in the Arctic.[10]

Rawl was the target of much of the criticism. At Exxon's May 1989 shareholders' meeting, he faced demonstrators outside the hall and angry stockholders within. Some of these demanded his resignation, and others suggested he donate some of his $1.4 million annual salary to the cleanup.

In response, Rawl acknowledged the corporation's "responsibility to clean up the spill and meet our obligations to those who were adversely affected by it." He promised an investigation of management's possible culpability and proposed the appointment of an environmentalist to the Exxon board. But about this latter pledge he admitted, "I don't know who that would be, and I don't know what the criteria would be."[11]

All these problems were logical outcomes of Exxon's haphazard response. Alternative approaches would have been helpful. For instance, a corporate communications officer at another company observed that Exxon "might have avoided many public relations problems if it had immediately communicated with its credit card customers about the situation in Alaska and cleanup efforts, if it had monitored reaction to [these] notifications, and had reacted accordingly."[12]

Another analyst noted that Exxon had failed to follow "Disaster Communications Rule #1: Quickly take charge of the news flow and give the public, by way of the news media, a credible, concerned and wholly committed spokesperson."[13] (This, of course, is what Johnson & Johnson had done in the person of chairman James Burke.)

The *New York Times* made a similar point: "The biggest mistake was that Exxon's chairman, Lawrence G. Rawl, sent a succession of lower-ranking executives to Alaska to deal with the spill instead of going there himself and taking control of the situation in a forceful, highly visible way. This gave the impression that the company regarded the pollution problem as not important enough to involve top management."[14]

Rawl himself soon recognized that Exxon's public relations response to the crisis had left much to be desired. In May 1989, he told *Fortune* magazine that "in hindsight, it would have helped" if he had been more visible during the first days following the spill.

When asked what advice he would offer to other CEOs, he said: "You'd better prethink which way you are going to jump from a public affairs standpoint before you have any kind of problem. You ought to always have a public affairs plan, even though it's kind of hard to force yourself to think in terms of a chemical plant blowing up or spilling all that oil in Prince William Sound."[15]

When Exxon finally tried to limit the damage being done to its corporate image, the company's public relations staff found itself playing catch-up against a skeptical press corps. For instance, widely disseminated pictures showed Exxon volunteers rescuing sea otters and birds from the oil slick, but news stories often were critical. *The New Republic* reported in September that "researchers now know that more than 800 sea otters died despite Exxon's well-publicized $8 million effort to rescue a few dozen. The scientists have found the carcasses of more than 28,000 sea birds, and they believe that the oil killed many times that number."[16] The liberal journal *The Nation* was even blunter when describing Exxon: "Unfortunately, virtually every assertion by the company is an outright lie or a deliberate distortion."[17]

Other Exxon efforts to win friends and influence opinion also were criticized. The company's payments to holders of commercial fishing permits did not reach many of the crew members whose livelihood was at least temporarily ruined. A $32,000 grant to the Alaska Public Radio Network, which had been a source for some national news organizations' coverage of the spill, was refused because it created at least the impression of a conflict of interest. Neil Conan, executive producer of National Public Radio's "All Things Considered," said, "We'd have had to say, 'This report on the oil spill was brought to you by a grant from Exxon,' and that would have been unacceptable."[18]

Even some of Exxon's friends ended up making life more difficult for the company. For example, White House Chief of Staff John Sununu criticized journalists for not paying more attention to the fact that more than one million barrels of oil did *not* escape from the Exxon Valdez. Not surprisingly, Sununu's pronouncement received sarcastic press treatment that reinforced public perceptions of Exxon as trying to dodge blame.[19]

Much of the Exxon response to the oil spill can be characterized as too little, too late, too sloppy. The absence of Rawl or another

high-profile spokesperson meant that there was "a vacuum that created confusion [and] mistrust."[20]

This nonfeasance led to the issue being defined by others whose
interests were far different from those of Exxon's executives. One
public relations practitioner noted: "The oil industry inexplicably
misjudged the rising public apprehension about environmental damage. Politicians and the media have not. They are always ready to
move in to fill the void—and they define who is to blame."[21]

The general rule about this is that "delay in attending to political communication can result in the formation of an irresistible
political force."[22] No enterprise wants its future to be determined by
such a force.

CRISIS LESSONS

Comparing the Tylenol and the Exxon Valdez crises and looking at
other similar events will underscore the importance of some fundamental public relations principles:

- Act promptly. Few crises vanish on their own. Delaying a
  response to events merely turns over control of the situation to
  someone else. If, for example, Johnson & Johnson had been as
  sluggish as Exxon was, news coverage certainly would have
  been more negative, and the Tylenol brand probably would
  have been beyond rescue.
- Recognize diverse publics' diverse interests. Consumers and the
  general public, employees, and stockholders view the crisis
  from different perspectives and have different stakes in the resolution of crisis-related problems. Each group merits a well-
  thought-out public relations strategy.

    For example, during the first Tylenol crisis, Johnson & John-
    son commissioned a daily telephone survey to monitor public
    opinion. This polling found that the public did not blame John-
    son & Johnson but remained fearful that the Tylenol on store
    shelves might have been poisoned. Company officials were con-
    vinced that product supplies around the country were safe, but,
    according to Burson-Marsteller and Johnson & Johnson docu-
    ments, "The company knew that by removing the product from

the shelf, it would be perceived as acting responsibly . . . a responsible company would remove it."[23] So, by implementing a heavily publicized recall of the product, Johnson & Johnson "moved the focus of the news coverage away from negative publicity about Tylenol and onto positive publicity about a corporation acting responsibly."[24]

The strong corporate image projected in such efforts was reassuring to stockholders and employees. Also, Johnson & Johnson made full use of its internal communications capabilities to keep employee morale high. This helped pave the way for the launching of the new, "safe-package" Tylenol soon thereafter.

- Establish an ethical credo and design a crisis plan in advance. Johnson & Johnson based its response on a long-standing corporate commitment to safeguard the public's interest. This was the company's stated philosophy long before the Tylenol incidents happened. The corporate response therefore was driven by good ethics, not merely by concern about the bottom line. As for advance crisis planning, Johnson & Johnson was lucky, Exxon was not. Neither had a comprehensive crisis plan in place when their respective crises happened. Johnson & Johnson benefited from smoother and wiser decision making, but its actions might have been even more effective had crisis situations been anticipated and responses designed. Not every catastrophe can be foreseen, but many can.

  An executive at chemical manufacturer Monsanto Corporation says: "The Exxon Valdez reaffirmed what we've already learned—that you must have a good crisis plan that's been carefully tested in the field to make sure it works under actual conditions." For instance, he says, "We did a drill at one of our plants in Ohio, and discovered that the fire department's radios operated on a different frequency than ours, severely hampering communications." He adds that every Monsanto plant's crisis plan is tested several times per year.[25]

- Understand news media operations. When the crisis story breaks, the corporate interests of a Johnson & Johnson or an Exxon are the last things that most news organizations care about. Coverage will proceed, regardless of whether it is aided, hindered, or ignored by the people with public relations responsibilities. Johnson & Johnson was helped during the Tylenol crisis because its public relations staff (which included former journalists) recognized the importance that news organizations attached to the story. The public relations practitioners were sensitive to reporters' deadline pressures and needs for information. Spokespersons were made available, calls were returned, and rapport was established between corporate officials and journalists. Such public relations professionalism is bound to benefit the client/employer.

In crisis situations, as the foregoing cases illustrate, the importance of ethical behavior by public relations practitioners is particularly important. Being an honest and forthright representative will meet the dual responsibilities of serving the needs of the client/employer and serving the public interest.

These cases also illustrate the need for a company to have in place an ethical foundation on which policy can be built during times of crisis.

More than normal, day-to-day work, crisis situations accelerate responses to public relations efforts. For instance, a deception, if found out, is likely to provoke an immediate, explosive reaction in the midst of a crisis. On the other hand, honesty will pay immediate dividends in the way public opinion develops. In the Tylenol and Exxon Valdez cases, public attitudes firmed up quickly—sympathetic toward Johnson & Johnson, angry about Exxon. These attitudes, which were largely a result of public relations efforts, had lasting impact on the public stature of both corporations.

The Tylenol case raises an issue that sometimes is overlooked. Johnson & Johnson received much acclaim for its response to the crisis, but the question may be asked: Does a company deserve an avalanche of praise for doing what it may be reasonably expected to do? Should acting in accord with social responsibility—social norms—elicit extraordinary applause?[26]

Perhaps part of the reason Johnson & Johnson's actions were greeted so effusively was that they were—or at least were perceived to be—exceptional. Much of the public and the press did not anticipate anything more than a cover-up attempt, and so when the corporation was forthcoming, its efforts were attributed largely to altruism. The notion, for example, that Johnson & Johnson may have been using its product recall as a shrewd marketing ploy received only limited scrutiny.

If one is willing to set aside cynicism about motives, the issue of social responsibility as social norm remains paramount. With that as the principal lesson of the Tylenol case, public relations practitioners should recognize that they can do much to make the public interest and their client/employer's interest coincide.

That is not just an ethical responsibility; it is also an ethical opportunity.

CHAPTER NINE

Toward a More Ethical Profession

Ethical behavior and successful public relations work can and should be wholly compatible.

The issues and cases discussed in this book indicate that the road to ethical professionalism is often steep and bumpy. Many ethical tests are faced by the public relations practitioner and the industry as a whole. All these challenges can be met if moral responsibility is acknowledged to be an integral part of this profession.

A chapter-by-chapter recapitulation of some of the findings of *Public Relations Ethics* underscores this mandate for responsibility.

As discussed in Chapter One, industrywide standards are useful, as are guidelines adopted by public relations firms and departments. But the keystone of an ethical profession is the individual practitioner. He or she must always keep in mind the influence that his or her work has, and match that influence with commensurate accountability.

Chapter Two underscores the need for a systematic way of responding to ethical responsibilities. Without codified standards, the disparate duties and diverse tasks that are part of public relations would be likely to overwhelm even the most conscientious practitioner. The needs and expectations of clients, requirements of law, standards of industry, and values of the individual all should be weighed, sorted, and shaped into a code of principles.

This process might not provide specific answers to every ethical question, but it will serve as a foundation for decision making. Without this, the practitioner would be forced to wing it, relying on wobbly situational ethics. That is asking for trouble.

The theories discussed in Chapter Three illustrate the intellectual sophistication from which a profession's ethical standards evolve.

Ethical behavior must meet the demands of the events of the moment, but it also must be grounded in theories that have been strengthened by passage of time.

Taking this philosophical base and integrating it into day-to-day business procedure is an essential bridge between theory and practice. As is discussed in Chapter Four, every stage of the relationship between practitioner and client/employer should reflect ethical considerations. How public relations professionals can *and should* represent their clients/employers ought to be carefully considered and thoroughly discussed so expectations will be set and performance will be evaluated according to measures that are reasonable and ethical.

Some of the difficulties of integrating ethics into business practices are portrayed in Chapter Five's analysis of definitions of "truth." Truth is the essence of ethical communication, but what exactly is it? Does telling the truth mean telling the *whole* truth, or are some omissions acceptable? Is selective emphasis truthful and ethical? The answer to such questions is a resounding "perhaps." But when selective use of facts causes harm to individuals or society collectively, the answer is more definitive: A breach of ethics has occurred.[1]

The overriding lesson of Chapter Six is that the relationship between public relations practitioners and news media representatives requires mutual respect and shared appreciation of the demands and responsibilities of both professions. News organizations are often essential conveyors of public relations information, but they also can be angry watchdogs if public relations efforts are perceived as straying beyond ethical bounds. These two professions have in common the business of communicating and so should also have in common many fundamental ethical standards.

Just as public relations practitioners often interact with journalists, so, too, do they frequently become involved in government and politics. Because maintaining the integrity of political and governmental processes is so important, the public relations practitioner's work as advocate (for candidate, institution, or cause) must meet rigorous tests of professional responsibility. An important lesson articulated in Chapter Seven is that the public relations practitioner can help replenish the always-short supply of truth in politics.

Truth also is a valuable, and sometimes scarce, commodity in times of crisis. Chapter Eight's examples of high-profile crisis public relations efforts underscore the importance of having ethical principles in mind constantly, however great the pressures of the moment might be. These cases illustrate that ethical public relations is good business practice. That, too, should always be kept in mind.

The findings of these chapters have their own intrinsic value and also serve as a foundation for building the public relations profession of the future. Ethical challenges are never static. They change as new cases arise and new thinking shapes attitudes. For example, "the growth of international media, global business and global politics has strengthened the role of international publics" and created the need to consider global ethics in organizational decision making.[2] Today's professionals face the demanding task of defining ethical principles for international practice.

Evolving communications technology also promises to necessitate new, sophisticated ethical standards. One issue fueling debate is the increased malleability of truth. For instance, computer software programs can make a photograph something much different from a mirror image of reality. It can enhance the finest points of a scene, making what had been almost invisible strikingly clear. Also, it can recompose the picture, removing a person from a photo or cloning a person to appear twice in the same shot. The computer easily performs far more complex tasks than traditional darkroom gear, and many alterations of the original image are almost impossible to detect.

With such capabilities at their disposal, public relations practitioners must resist the temptation to "improve upon" the truth. Ethical guidelines must be revised frequently to keep pace with ever-changing technology.

Along similar lines, many public relations practitioners increasingly use video news releases rather than the printed word to deliver their messages. Availability of this glitzier format should not foster diminished regard for accuracy. This is particularly important because the videotape might not be subjected to the same editorial scrutiny as the printed release. Reediting videotape is often harder than rewriting print copy. So TV stations—particularly small ones—may be tempted to air all or part of the video release as is.

With the proliferation of local cable television stations, the appetite for ready-to-air material will keep growing. Also, the launching within the next few years of hundreds of new communications satellites means public relations professionals, like other communicators, will have more access to more publics. That also means communicators should be prepared to shoulder more ethical responsibility.

Sophisticated home computers, fax machines, and other such gear also will enhance access. This means greater reliance will be placed on public relations messages in their original form; they will more often reach their audiences directly, unscreened by intermediaries such as the news media.

These photography, television, and other issues provide a look at just several facets of technology-driven ethics. The public relations practitioner need not be a science junkie to appreciate the magnitude of changes taking place and to recognize the ethical challenges that will accompany these changes.

As the public relations industry is transformed, so, too, will training and qualifications evolve for those who practice this trade. Most of the men and women who enter the field will have received sophisticated schooling in public relations per se—something that was unheard of when the profession took shape during the first half of this century. Client and public expectations will keep rising, and rightly so.

The future of the profession is inextricably linked to public relations education. In addition to having skills such as writing and campaign planning, the true professional should have a good understanding of the *philosophy* of public relations. That philosophy should include solid grounding in the theory and practice of ethics.

The importance of such training cannot be overstated. Ultimately, with or without a code of conduct, "those who practice public relations must *choose* to be ethical because they believe in themselves and want others to respect them."[3]

On a broad scale, public relations communicators—whether representing their own or others' interests—are increasingly seen as arbiters of professional standards. Susan Fry Bovet, editor of *Public Relations Journal*, described the issue this way:

> It's arguable that every question of business ethics that comes to light in the press is a public relations issue, since the organization's reputation is at stake. So in a large sense, every business scandal involves the public relations field and its practitioners. Even closer to home, there is the question of appropriate conduct

of public relations as a business and the appropriate practice of public relations in organizations of all kinds, including for-profit organizations, the military, nonprofit groups and even charities.[4]

This spectrum of issues is challenging in part because of its scope and in part because of the intellectual complexity of its constituent parts.

Regardless of the difficulty of this challenge, it must be met. In our communications society, the pervasiveness and influence of public relations necessitate that it be practiced ethically.

Public relations *does* matter.

Appendix

**CODE OF PROFESSIONAL STANDARDS
FOR THE PRACTICE OF PUBLIC RELATIONS
PUBLIC RELATIONS SOCIETY OF AMERICA**

**COUNSELORS ACADEMY INTERPRETATION
TO THE PRSA CODE OF
PROFESSIONAL STANDARDS**

**INTERNATIONAL BILL OF RIGHTS OF THE
UNITED NATIONS UNIVERSAL DECLARATION
OF HUMAN RIGHTS**

**INTERNATIONAL PUBLIC RELATIONS
ASSOCIATION CODE OF ETHICS
CODE OF ATHENS**

**INTERNATIONAL ASSOCIATION OF
BUSINESS COMMUNICATORS'
CODE OF ETHICS**

CODE OF PROFESSIONAL STANDARDS FOR THE PRACTICE OF PUBLIC RELATIONS*

Public Relations Society of America

This Code was adapted by the PRSA Assembly in 1988. It replaces a Code of Ethics in force since 1950 and revised in 1954, 1959, 1963, 1977, and 1983. For information on the Code and enforcement procedures, please call the chair of the Board of Ethics through PRSA Headquarters.

Declaration of Principles

Members of the Public Relations Society of America base their professional principles on the fundamental value and dignity of the individual, holding that the free exercise of human rights, especially freedom of speech, freedom of assembly, and freedom of the press, is essential to the practice of public relations.

In serving the interests of clients and employers, we dedicate ourselves to the goals of better communication, understanding, and cooperation among the diverse individuals, groups, and institutions of society, and of equal opportunity of employment to the public relations profession.

We pledge:
To conduct ourselves professionally, with truth, accuracy, fairness, and responsibility to the public;

To improve our individual competence and advance the knowledge and proficiency of the profession through continuing research and education;

And to adhere to the articles of the Code of Professional Standards for the Practice of Public Relations as adopted by the governing Assembly of the Society.

Code of Professional Standards for the Practice of Public Relations

These articles have been adopted by the Public Relations Society of America to promote and maintain high standards of public service and ethical conduct among its members.

Reprinted with permission of the Public Relations Society of America.

1. A member shall conduct his or her professional life in accord with the **public interest**.

2. A member shall exemplify high standards of **honesty and integrity** while carrying out dual obligations to a client or employer and to the democratic process.

3. A member shall **deal fairly** with the public, with past or present clients or employers, and with fellow practitioners, giving due respect to the ideal of free inquiry and to the opinions of others.

4. A member shall adhere to the highest standards of **accuracy and truth**, avoiding extravagant claims or unfair comparisons and giving credit for ideas and words borrowed from others.

5. A member shall not knowingly disseminate **false or misleading information** and shall act promptly to correct erroneous communications for which he or she is responsible.

6. A member shall not engage in any practice which has the purpose of **corrupting** the integrity of channels of communications or the processes of government.

7. A member shall be prepared to **identify publicly** the name of the client or employer on whose behalf any public communication is made.

8. A member shall not use any individual or organization professing to serve or represent an announced cause, or professing to be independent or unbiased, but actually serving another or **undisclosed interest**.

9. A member shall not **guarantee the achievement** of specified results beyond the member's direct control.

10. A member shall **not represent conflicting** or competing interests without the express consent of those concerned, given after a full disclosure of the facts.

11. A member shall not place himself or herself in a position where the member's **personal interest is or may be in conflict** with an obligation to an employer or client, or others, without full disclosure of such interests to all involved.

12. A member shall **not accept fees, commissions, gifts or any other consideration** from anyone except clients or employers for whom services are performed without their express consent, given after full disclosure of the facts.

13. A member shall scrupulously safeguard the **confidences and privacy rights** of present, former, and prospective clients or employers.

14. A member shall not intentionally **damage the professional reputation** or practice of another practitioner.

15. If a member has evidence that another member has been guilty of unethical, illegal, or unfair practices, including those in violation of this Code, the member is obligated to present the information promptly to the proper authorities of the Society for action in accordance with the procedure set forth in Article XII of the Bylaws.

16. A member called as a witness in a proceeding for enforcement of this Code is obligated to appear, unless excused for sufficient reason by the judicial panel.

17. A member shall, as soon as possible, sever relations with any organization or individual if such relationship requires conduct contrary to the articles of this Code.

Official Interpretations of the Code

Interpretation of Code Paragraph 1, which reads, "A member shall conduct his or her professional life in accord with the public interest."

The public interest is here defined primarily as comprising respect for and enforcement of the rights guaranteed by the Constitution of the United States of America.

Interpretation of Code Paragraph 6, which reads, "A member shall not engage in any practice which has the purpose of corrupting the integrity of channels of communication or the processes of government."

1. Among the practices prohibited by this paragraph are those that tend to place representatives of media or government under any obligation to the member, or the member's employer or client, which is in conflict with their obligations to media or government, such as:

   a. the giving of gifts of more than nominal value;

   b. any form of payment or compensation to a member of the media in order to obtain preferential or guaranteed news or editorial coverage in the medium;

    c.   any retainer or fee to a media employee or use of such employee if retained by a client or employer, where the circumstances are not fully disclosed to and accepted by the media employer;

    d.   providing trips, for media representatives, that are unrelated to legitimate news interests;

    e.   the use by a member of an investment or loan or advertising commitment made by the member, or the member's client or employer, to obtain preferential or guaranteed coverage in the medium.

2. This Code paragraph does not prohibit hosting media or government representatives at meals, cocktails, or news functions and special events that are occasions for the exchange of news information or views, or the furtherance of understanding, which is part of the public relations function. Nor does it prohibit the bona fide press event or tour when media or government representatives are given the opportunity for an on-the-spot viewing of a newsworthy product, process, or event in which the media or government representatives have a legitimate interest. What is customary or reasonable hospitality has to be a matter of particular judgment in specific situations. In all of these cases, however, it is, or should be, understood that no preferential treatment or guarantees are expected or implied and that complete independence always is left to the media or government representative.

3. This paragraph does not prohibit the reasonable giving or lending of sample products or services to media representatives who have a legitimate interest in the products or services.

4. It is permissible, under Article 6 of the Code, to offer complimentary or discount rates to the media (travel writers, for example) if the rate is for business use and is made available to all writers. Considerable question exists as to the propriety of extending such rates for personal use.

Interpretation of Code Paragraph 9, which reads, "A member shall not guarantee the achievement of specified results beyond the member's direct control."

This Code paragraph, in effect, prohibits misleading a client or employer as to what professional public relations can accomplish. It does not prohibit guarantees of quality or service. But it does prohibit guaranteeing specific results which, by their very nature, cannot be guaranteed because they are not subject to the member's control. As an example, a guarantee that a news release will appear specifically in a particular publication would be prohibited. This paragraph should not be interpreted as prohibiting contingent fees.

Interpretation of Code Paragraph 13, which reads, "A member shall scrupulously safeguard the confidences and privacy rights of present, former, and prospective clients or employers."

1. This article does not prohibit a member who has knowledge of client or employer activities that are illegal from making such disclosures to the proper authorities as he or she believes are legally required.
2. Communications between a practitioner and client/employer are deemed to be confidential under Article 13 of the Code of Professional Standards. However, although practitioner/client/employer communications are considered confidential between the parties, such communications are not privileged against disclosure in a court of law.
3. Under the copyright laws of the United States, the copyright in a work is generally owned initially by the author or authors. In the case of a "work made for hire" by an employee acting within the scope of his or her employment, the employer is considered to be the author and owns the copyright in the absence of an express, signed written agreement to the contrary. A freelancer who is the author of the work and is not an employee may be the owner of the copyright. A member should consult legal counsel for detailed advice concerning the scope and application of the copyright laws.

Interpretation of Code Paragraph 14, which reads, "A member shall not intentionally damage the professional reputation or practice of another practitioner."

1. Blind solicitation, on its face, is not prohibited by the Code. However, if the customer list were improperly obtained, or if

the solicitation contained references reflecting adversely on the quality of current services, a complaint might be justified.

2. This article applies to statements, true or false, or acts, made or undertaken with malice and with the specific purpose of harming the reputation or practice of another member. This article does not prohibit honest employee evaluations or similar reviews, made without malice and as part of ordinary business practice, even though this activity may have a harmful effect.

An Official Interpretation of the Code as It Applies to Political Public Relations

Preamble

In the practice of political public relations, a PRSA member must have professional capabilities to offer an employer or client quite apart from any political relationships of value, and members may serve their employer or client without necessarily having attributed to them the character, reputation, or beliefs of those they serve. It is understood that members may choose to serve only those interests with whose political philosophy they are personally comfortable.

Definition.

"Political Public Relations" is defined as those areas of public relations that relate to:

a. the counseling of political organizations, committees, candidates, or potential candidates for public office; and groups constituted for the purpose of influencing the vote on any ballot issue;

b. the counseling of holders of public office;

c. the management, or direction, of a political campaign for or against a candidate for political office; or for or against a ballot issue to be determined by voter approval or rejection;

d. the practice of public relations on behalf of a client or an employer in connection with that client's or employer's relationships with any candidates or holders of public office, with the purpose of influencing legislation or government regulation or treatment of a client or employer, regardless of whether the PRSA member is a recognized lobbyist;

e. the counseling of government bodies, or segments thereof, either domestic or foreign.

Precepts.

1. It is the responsibility of PRSA members practicing political public relations, as defined above, to be conversant with the various statutes, local, state, and federal, governing such activities and to adhere to them strictly. This includes, but is not limited to, the various local, state, and federal laws, court decisions, and official interpretations governing lobbying, political contributions, disclosure, elections, libel, slander, and the like. In carrying out this responsibility, members shall seek appropriate counseling whenever necessary.

2. It is also the responsibility of the members to abide by PRSA's Code of Professional Standards.

3. Members shall represent clients or employers in good faith, and while partisan advocacy on behalf of a candidate or public issue may be expected, members shall act in accord with the public interest and adhere to truth and accuracy and to generally accepted standards of good taste.

4. Members shall not issue descriptive material or any advertising or publicity information or participate in the preparation or use thereof that is not signed by responsible persons or is false, misleading, or unlabeled as to its source, and are obligated to use care to avoid dissemination of any such material.

5. Members have an obligation to clients to disclose what remuneration beyond their fees they expect to receive as a result of their relationship, such as commissions for media advertising, printing, and the like, and should not accept such extra payment without their client's consent.

6. Members shall not improperly use their positions to encourage additional future employment or compensation. It is understood that successful campaign directors or managers, because of the performance of their duties and the working relationship that develops, may well continue to assist and counsel, for pay, the successful candidate.

7. Members shall voluntarily disclose to employers or clients the identity of other employers or clients with whom they are currently associated, and whose interests might be affected favorably or unfavorably by their political representation.
8. Members shall respect the confidentiality of information pertaining to employers or clients past, present, and potential, even after the relationships cease, avoiding future associations wherein insider information is sought that would give a desired advantage over a member's previous clients.
9. In avoiding practices that might tend to corrupt the processes of government, members shall not make undisclosed gifts of cash or other valuable considerations that are designed to influence specific decisions of voters, legislators, or public officials on public matters. A business lunch or dinner, or other comparable expenditure made in the course of communicating a point of view or public position, would not constitute such a violation. Nor, for example, would a plant visit designed and financed to provide useful background information to an interested legislator or candidate.
10. Nothing herein should be construed as prohibiting members from making legal, properly disclosed contributions to the candidates, party, or referenda issues of their choice.
11. Members shall not, through use of information known to be false or misleading, conveyed directly or through a third party, intentionally injure the public reputation of an opposing interest.

An Official Interpretation of the Code as It Applies to Financial Public Relations

This interpretation of the Society Code as it applies to financial public relations was originally adopted in 1963 and amended in 1972, 1977, 1983 and 1988 by action of the PRSA Board of Directors. "Financial public relations" is defined as "that area of public relations which relates to the dissemination of information that affects the understanding of stockholders and investors generally concerning the financial position and prospects of a company, and includes among its objectives the improvement of relations between corporations and their stockholders." The interpretation was prepared in

1963 by the Society's Financial Relations Committee, working with the Securities and Exchange Commission and with the advice of the Society's legal counsel. It is rooted directly in the Code with the full force of the Code behind it, and a violation of any of the following paragraphs is subject to the same procedures and penalties as violation of the Code.

1. It is the responsibility of PRSA members who practice financial public relations to be thoroughly familiar with and understand the rules and regulations of the SEC and the laws it administers, as well as other laws, rules, and regulations affecting financial public relations, and to act in accordance with their letter and spirit. In carrying out this responsibility, members shall also seek legal counsel, when appropriate, on matters concerning financial public relations.
2. Members shall adhere to the general policy of making full and timely disclosure of corporate information on behalf of clients or employers. The information disclosed shall be accurate, clear, and understandable. The purpose of such disclosure is to provide the investing public with all material information affecting security values or influencing investment decisions. In complying with the duty of full and timely disclosure, members shall present all material facts, including those adverse to the company. They shall exercise care to ascertain the facts and to disseminate only information they believe to be accurate. They shall not knowingly omit information, the omission of which might make a release false or misleading. Under no circumstances shall members participate in any activity designed to mislead or manipulate the price of a company's securities.
3. Members shall publicly disclose or release information promptly so as to avoid the possibility of any use of the information by any insider or third party. To that end, members shall make every effort to comply with the spirit and intent of the timely-disclosure policies of the stock exchanges, NASD, and the SEC. Material information shall be made available on an equal basis.
4. Members shall not disclose confidential information the disclosure of which might be adverse to a valid corporate

purpose or interest and whose disclosure is not required by the timely-disclosure provisions of the law. During any such period of nondisclosure members shall not directly or indirectly (a) communicate the confidential information to any other person or (b) buy or sell or in any other way deal in the company's securities where the confidential information may materially affect the market for the security when disclosed. Material information shall be disclosed publicly as soon as its confidential status has terminated or the requirement of timely disclosure takes effect.

5. During the registration period, members shall not engage in practices designed to precondition the market of such securities. During registration, the issuance of forecasts, projections, predictions about sales and earnings, or opinions concerning security values or other aspects of the future performance of the company, shall be in accordance with current SEC regulations and statements of policy. In the case of companies whose securities are publicly held, the normal flow of factual information to shareholders and the investing public shall continue during the registration period.

6. Where members have any reason to doubt that projections have an adequate basis in fact, they shall satisfy themselves as to the adequacy of the projections prior to disseminating them.

7. Acting in concert with clients or employers, members shall act promptly to correct false or misleading information or rumors concerning clients' or employers' securities or business whenever they have reason to believe such information or rumors are materially affecting investor attitudes.

8. Members shall not issue descriptive materials designed or written in such a fashion as to appear to be, contrary to fact, an independent third-party endorsement or recommendation of a company or a security. Whenever members issue material for clients or employers, either in their own names or in the names of someone other than the clients or employers, they shall disclose in large type and in a prominent position on the face of the material the source of such material and the existence of the issuer's client or employer relationship.

9. Members shall not use inside information for personal gain. However, this is not intended to prohibit members from making bona fide investments in their company's or client's securities insofar as they can make such investments without the benefit of material inside information.

10. Members shall not accept compensation that would place them in a position of conflict with their duty to a client, employer, or the investing public. Members shall not accept stock options from clients or employers nor accept securities as compensation at a price below market price except as part of an overall plan for corporate employees.

11. Members shall act so as to maintain the integrity of channels of public communication. They shall not pay or permit to be paid to any publication or other communications medium any consideration in exchange for publicizing a company, except through clearly recognizable paid advertising.

12. Members shall in general be guided by the PRSA Declaration of Principles and the Code of Professional Standards for the Practice of Public Relations of which this is an official interpretation.

COUNSELORS ACADEMY INTERPRETATION TO THE PRSA CODE OF PROFESSIONAL STANDARDS*

Members of counseling firms have a specific responsibility to maintain the highest standards of ethics in the practice of public relations. Counselors embrace the many responsibilities of serving the interests of clients and the public at large, while considering their own personal interests and those of their firms. There are several key relationships in every public relations counseling business, and they involve:

- clients we serve;
- each other, as employees and competitors;
- media with whom we work;
- suppliers with whom we work;
- communities where we live and work.

Reprinted with permission of the Public Relations Society of America.

Members of the Counselors Academy, and each member's employees, are expected to practice his or her profession in the most responsible, reliable, truthful and cooperative way.

The Counselors Academy advocates the following precepts:

1. Counselors have an overriding responsibility to carefully balance public interests with those of their clients, and to place both those interests above their own.
2. Counselors must operate in an open and truthful manner at all times.
3. Counselors have a responsibility to protect the integrity of certain elements of public relations practice, including:
   - contracts and non-compete agreements between counseling firms and their employees,
   - contracts and agreements between counseling firms and clients,
   - confidential client information, and
   - confidential agency information.
4. It is incumbent on counselors to understand the requirements to their clients and to exert best efforts to satisfy those requirements by submitting realistic proposals on performance, cost and schedule. Counselors will employ the highest ethical business practices in source selection, negotiation, determination of awards and the administration of all purchasing activities.
5. Counselors must not work for more than one client or employer whose goals may be in conflict, without the express consent of those concerned, given after a full disclosure of the facts. Members must be particularly sensitive to alleviate situations where a conflict of interest or even a perception of such a conflict could originate.
6. Counselors must not collect fees for services based on guaranteed results of any kind with media or other third parties.
7. Counselors have an obligation to clients to disclose any remuneration beyond their fees that they expect to receive as a result of their relationship, and should not accept such extra payments without their client's consent.

8. Counselors shall respect the confidentiality of information pertaining to present, former and prospective clients, and avoid future associations wherein insider information is used that would give a desired advantage over the counselor's previous clients.

9. In no instance may counselors use or share inside information, which is not otherwise available to the general public, for any manner of personal gain as might be realized, for example, through trading in the stock of a client company.

10. We consider that it could be a breach of our standards for any counseling firm to seek a competitive advantage through the payment or receipt of extraordinary gifts, gratuities, or other favors.

11. Counselors shall not personally, or in the interests of a client, intentionally injure the public reputation of another practitioner.

12. Counselors must move quickly to present evidence of unethical activity by other counselors to the proper authorities of the Society.

13. Counselors shall in general be guided by the PRSA Declaration of Principles and the PRSA Code of Professional Standards for the Practice of Public Relations of which this document is an interpretation.

The Committee on Business Practices

The Counselors Academy
Public Relations Society of America

October 1990

INTERNATIONAL BILL OF RIGHTS OF THE UNITED NATIONS

Universal Declaration of Human Rights

Preamble

Whereas recognition of the inherent dignity and of the equal and inalienable rights of all members of the human family is the foundation of freedom, justice and peace in the world,

Whereas disregard and contempt for human rights have resulted in barbarous acts which have outraged the conscience of mankind, and the advent of a world in which human beings shall enjoy freedom of speech and belief and freedom from fear and want has been proclaimed as the highest aspiration of the common people,

Whereas it is essential, if man is not to be compelled to have recourse, as a last resort, to rebellion against tyranny and oppression, that human rights should be protected by the rule of law,

Whereas it is essential to promote the development of friendly relations between nations,

Whereas the people of the United Nations have in the Charter reaffirmed their faith in fundamental human rights, in the dignity and worth of the human person and in the equal rights of men and women and have determined to promote social progress and better standards of life in larger freedom,

Whereas Member States have pledged themselves to achieve, in cooperation with the United Nations, the promotion of universal respect for and observance of human rights and fundamental freedoms,

Whereas a common understanding of these rights and freedoms is of the greatest importance for the full realizations of this pledge,

Now, therefore,

The General Assembly

Proclaims this Universal Declaration of Human Rights as a common standard of achievement for all peoples and all nations, to the end that every individual and every organ of society, keeping this Declaration constantly in mind, shall strive by teaching and education to promote respect for these rights and freedoms and by progressive measures, national and international, to secure their universal and effective recognition and observance, both among the peoples of Member States themselves and among the peoples of territories under their jurisdiction.

Article 1

All human beings are born free and equal in dignity and rights. They are endowed with reason and conscience and should act towards one another in a spirit of brotherhood.

Article 2

Everyone is entitled to all the rights and freedoms set forth in this Declaration, without distinction of any kind, such as race, colour, sex, language, religion, political or other opinion, national or social origin, property, birth or other status.

Furthermore, no distinction shall be made on the basis of the political, jurisdictional or international status of the country or territory to which a person belongs, whether it be independent, trust, non-self-governing or under any other limitation of sovereignty.

Article 3

Everyone has the right to life, liberty and security of person.

Article 4

No one shall be held in slavery or servitude; slavery and the slave trade shall be prohibited in all their forms.

Article 5

No one shall be subjected to torture or to cruel, inhuman or degrading treatment or punishment.

Article 6

Everyone has the right to recognition everywhere as a person before the law.

Article 7

All are equal before the law and are entitled without any discrimination to equal protection of the law. All are entitled to equal protection against any discrimination in violation of this Declaration and against any incitement to such discrimination.

Article 8

Everyone has the right to an effective remedy by the competent national tribunals for acts violating the fundamental rights granted him by the constitution or by law.

Article 9

No one shall be subjected to arbitrary arrest, detention or exile.

Article 10

Everyone is entitled in full equality to a fair and public hearing by an independent and impartial tribunal, in the determination of his rights and obligations and of any criminal charge against him.

Article 11

1. Everyone charged with a penal offence has the right to be presumed innocent until proved guilty according to law in a public trial at which he has had all the guarantees necessary for his defence.

2. No one shall be held guilty of any penal offence on account of any act or omission which did not constitute a penal offence, under national or international law, at the time when it was committed. Nor shall a heavier penalty be imposed than the one that was applicable at the time the penal offence was committed.

Article 12

No one shall be subjected to arbitrary interference with his privacy, family, home or correspondence, nor to attacks upon his honour and reputation. Everyone has the right to the protection of the law against such interference or attacks.

Article 13

1. Everyone has the right to freedom of movement and residence within the borders of each State.

2. Everyone has the right to leave any country, including his own, and to return to his country.

Article 14

1. Everyone has the right to seek and to enjoy in other countries asylum from persecution.

2. This right may not be invoked in the case of prosecutions genuinely arising from non-political crimes or from acts contrary to the purposes and principles of the United Nations.

Article 15

1. Everyone has the right to a nationality.

2. No one shall be arbitrarily deprived of his nationality nor denied the right to change his nationality.

Article 16

1. Men and women of full age, without any limitation due to race, nationality or religion, have the right to marry and to found a family. They are entitled to equal rights as to marriage, during marriage and at its dissolution.
2. Marriage shall be entered into only with the free and full consent of the intending spouses.
3. The family is the natural and fundamental group unit of society and is entitled to protection by society and the State.

Article 17

1. Everyone has the right to own property alone as well as in association with others.
2. No one shall be arbitrarily deprived of his property.

Article 18

Everyone has the right to freedom of thought, conscience and religion; this right includes freedom to change his religion or belief, and freedom, either alone or in community with others and in public or private, to manifest his religion or belief in teaching, practice, worship and observance.

Article 19

Everyone has the right to freedom of opinion and expression; this right includes freedom to hold opinions without interference and to seek, receive and impart information and ideas through any media and regardless of frontiers.

Article 20

1. Everyone has the right to freedom of peaceful assembly and association.
2. No one may be compelled to belong to an association.

Article 21

1. Everyone has the right to take part in the government of his country, directly or through freely chosen representatives.

2. Everyone has the right of equal access to public service in his country.
3. The will of the people shall be the basis of the authority of government; this will shall be expressed in periodic and genuine elections which shall be by universal and equal suffrage and shall be held by secret vote or by equivalent free voting procedures.

Article 22

Everyone, as a member of society, has the right to social security and is entitled to realization, through national effort and international cooperation and in accordance with the organization and resources of each State, of the economic, social and cultural rights indispensable for his dignity and the free development of his personality.

Article 23

1. Everyone has the right to work, to free choice of employment, to just and favourable conditions of work and to protection against unemployment.
2. Everyone, without any discrimination, has the right to equal pay for equal work.
3. Everyone who works has the right to just and favourable remuneration ensuring for himself and his family an existence worthy of human dignity, and supplemented, if necessary, by the other means of social protection.
4. Everyone has the right to form and to join trade unions for the protection of his interests.

Article 24

Everyone has the right to rest and leisure, including reasonable limitation of working hours and periodic holidays with pay.

Article 25

1. Everyone has the right to a standard of living adequate for the health and well-being of himself and his family, including food, clothing, housing and medical care and necessary social services, and the right to security in the event of unemployment, sickness, disability, widowhood, old age or other lack of livelihood in circumstances beyond his control.

2. Motherhood and childhood are entitled to special care and assistance. All children, whether born in or out of wedlock, shall enjoy the same social protection.

Article 26

1. Everyone has the right to education. Education shall be free, at least in the elementary and fundamental stages. Elementary education shall be compulsory. Technical and professional education shall be made generally available and higher education shall be equally accessible to all on the basis of merit.
2. Education shall be directed to the full development of the human personality and to the strengthening of respect for human rights and fundamental freedoms. It shall promote understanding, tolerance and friendship among all nations, racial or religious groups, and shall further the activities of the United Nations for the maintenance of peace.
3. Parents have a prior right to choose the kind of education that shall be given to their children.

Article 27

1. Everyone has the right freely to participate in the cultural life of the community, to enjoy the arts and to share in scientific advancement and its benefits.
2. Everyone has the right to the protection of the moral and material interests resulting from any scientific, literary or artistic production of which he is the author.

Article 28

Everyone is entitled to a social and international order in which the rights and freedoms set forth in this Declaration can be fully realized.

Article 29

1. Everyone has duties to the community in which alone the free and full development of his personality is possible.
2. In the exercise of his rights and freedoms, everyone shall be subject only to such limitations as are determined by law solely for the purpose of securing due recognition and respect for the rights and freedoms of others and of meeting the just

requirements of morality, public order and the general welfare in a democratic society.

3. These rights and freedoms may in no case be exercised contrary to the purposes and principles of the United Nations.

Article 30

Nothing in this Declaration may be interpreted as implying for any State, group or person any right to engage in any activity or to perform any act aimed at the destruction of any of the rights and freedoms set forth herein.

INTERNATIONAL PUBLIC RELATIONS ASSOCIATION*

International Code of Ethics
Code of Athens

The English Version adopted by IPRA General Assembly at Athens on May 12, 1965, and modified at Tehran on April 17, 1968

CONSIDERING that all Member countries of the United Nations Organisation have agreed to abide by its Charter which reaffirms "its faith in fundamental human rights, in the dignity and worth of the human person" and that having regard to the very nature of their professions, Public Relations practitioners in these countries should undertake to ascertain and observe the principles set out in this Charter;

CONSIDERING that, apart from "rights," human beings have not only physical or material needs but also intellectual, moral and social needs and that their rights are of real benefit to them only in so far as these needs are essentially met;

CONSIDERING that, in the course of their professional duties and depending on how these duties are performed, Public Relations practitioners can substantially help to meet these intellectual, moral and social needs;

And lastly, CONSIDERING that the use of techniques enabling them to come simultaneously into contact with millions of people gives Public Relations practitioners a power that has to be restrained by the observance of a strict moral code.

*Reprinted with permission of the International Public Relations Association.

On all these grounds, the undersigned Public Relations Associations hereby declare that they accept as their moral charter the principles of the following Code of Ethics, and that if, in the light of evidence submitted to the Council, a member of these associations should be found to have infringed this Code in the course of his/her professional duties, he/she will be deemed to be guilty of serious misconduct calling for an appropriate penalty.

Accordingly, each Member of these Associations:

Shall Endeavour

1. To contribute to the achievement of the moral and cultural conditions enabling human beings to reach their full stature and enjoy the indefeasible rights to which they are entitled under the "Universal Declaration of Human Rights";
2. To establish communication patterns and channels which, by fostering the free flow of essential information, will make each member of the group feel that he/she is being kept informed, and also give him/her an awareness of his/her own personal involvement and responsibility, and of his/her solidarity with other members;
3. To conduct himself/herself always and in all circumstances in such a manner as to deserve and secure the confidence of those with whom he/she comes into contact;
4. To bear in mind that, because of the relationship between his/her profession and the public, his/her conduct—even in private—will have an impact on the way in which the profession as a whole is appraised.

Shall Undertake

5. To observe, in the course of his/her professional duties, the moral principles and rules of the "Universal Declaration of Human Rights";
6. To pay due regard to, and uphold, human dignity, and to recognise the right of each individual to judge for himself/herself;
7. To establish the moral, psychological and intellectual conditions for dialogue in its true sense, and to recognize the right

of the parties involved to state their case and express their views;

8. To act, in all circumstances, in such a manner as to take account of the respective interests of the parties involved: both the interests of the organisation which he/she serves and the interests of the publics concerned;

9. To carry out his/her undertakings and commitments, which shall always be so worded as to avoid any misunderstandings, and to show loyalty and integrity in all circumstances so as to keep the confidence of his/her clients or employers, past or present, and of all the publics that are affected by his/her actions.

Shall Refrain From

10. Subordinating the truth to other requirements;

11. Circulating information which is not based on established and ascertainable facts;

12. Taking part in any venture or undertaking which is unethical or dishonest or capable of impairing human dignity and integrity;

13. Using any "manipulative" methods or techniques designed to create subconscious motivations which the individual cannot control of his/her own free will and so cannot be held accountable for the action taken on them.

INTERNATIONAL ASSOCIATION OF BUSINESS COMMUNICATORS*

The IABC Code of Ethics has been developed to provide IABC members and other communication professionals with guidelines of professional behavior and standards of ethical practice. The Code will be reviewed and revised as necessary by the Ethics Committee and the Executive Board.

Any IABC member who wishes advice and guidance regarding its interpretation and/or application may write or phone IABC headquarters. Questions will be routed to the Executive Board member responsible for the Code.

*Reprinted courtesy International Association of Business Communicators.

Communication and Information Dissemination

1. *Communication professionals will uphold the credibility and dignity of their profession by encouraging the practice of honest, candid and timely communication.*

   The highest standards of professionalism will be upheld in all communication. Communicators should encourage frequent communication and messages that are honest in their content, candid, accurate and appropriate to the needs of the organization and its audiences.

2. *Professional communicators will not use any information that has been generated or appropriately acquired by a business for another business without permission. Further, communicators should attempt to identify the source of information to be used.*

   When one is changing employers, information developed at the previous position will not be used without permission from that employer. Acts of plagiarism and copyright infringement are illegal acts; material in the public domain should have its source attributed if possible. If an organization grants permission to use its information and requests public acknowledgment, it will be made in a place appropriate to the material used. The material will be used only for the purpose for which permission was granted.

Standards of Conduct

3. *Communication professionals will abide by the spirit and letter of all laws and regulations governing their professional activities.*

   All international, national and local laws and regulations must be observed, with particular attention to those pertaining to communication, such as copyright law. Industry and organizational regulations will also be observed.

4. *Communication professionals will not condone any illegal or unethical act related to their professional activity, their organization and its business or the public environment in which it operates.*

It is the personal responsibility of professional communicators to act honestly, fairly and with integrity at all times in all professional activities. Looking the other way while others act illegally tacitly condones such acts whether or not the communicator has committed them. The communicator should speak with the individual involved, his or her supervisor or appropriate authorities—depending on the context of the situation and one's own ethical judgment.

Confidentiality/Disclosure

5. *Communication professionals will respect the confidentiality and right-to-privacy of all individuals, employers, clients and customers.*

   Communicators must determine the ethical balance between right-to-privacy and need-to-know. Unless the situation involves illegal or grossly unethical acts, confidences should be maintained. If there is a conflict between right-to-privacy and need-to-know, a communicator should first talk with the source and negotiate the need for the information to be communicated.

6. *Communication professionals will not use any confidential information gained as a result of professional activity for personal benefit or for that of others.*

   Confidential information can not be used to give inside advantage to stock transactions, gain favors from outsiders, assist a competing company for whom one is going to work, assist companies in developing a marketing advantage, achieve a publishing advantage or otherwise act to the detriment of an organization. Such information must remain confidential during and after one's employment period.

Professionalism

7. *Communication professionals should uphold IABC's standards for ethical conduct in all professional activity, and should use IABC and its designation of accreditation (ABC) only for purposes that are authorized and fairly represent the organization and its professional standards.*

IABC recognizes the need for professional integrity within any organization, including the association. Members should acknowledge that their actions reflect on themselves, their organizations and their profession.

A System of Enactment

To guide communication professionals in ethical matters and assure professional consistency, an ethical philosophy and code must have a means of enactment. The code must reinforce the observance of all civil and criminal laws and regulations, yet be flexible enough for situational considerations and for seeking reform through legitimate channels.

Therefore, the following steps should be undertaken to enact the IABC Code of Ethics:

Communication

The code should be published, along with supplementary materials and a brief reference bibliography, in a folder given to each member on a one-time basis. New members should automatically receive a Code on joining.

Include a sentence on all application and annual renewal forms stating "I have reviewed and pledge to uphold IABC's code of ethics and standards of professional communication."

In all IABC application materials and introductory brochures, include the principles of the code.

Communication World should run an article on a topic of professional ethics relevant to IABC's philosophy at least annually. A variety of themes can be chosen from the code's principles and explanations. Different approaches and case examples can increase editorial options.

At least one session about ethics should be scheduled at the IABC annual conference to assist newer professionals in developing and refining their communication ethics, education and professional development. Ethics should also be supported in IABC's professional development seminar series and sessions at district conferences. Names of speakers on ethics should be made available and shared among districts and local chapters.

IABC ethics must be participatory. In the development of a communication ethos, two-way communication is essential; therefore, the proposed IABC ethics documents should be submitted for review by all chapters with feedback collected and discussed by the districts and sent to IABC. Clarification, specific questions and concerns with accompanying recommendations are important in developing a document that fairly and honestly represents the ethical perspective of its membership. Above all, the opinions and concerns of members in *all* countries must be given full consideration.

Review Committee

Establish an ethics review committee of at least three accredited members. Non-accredited members may be appointed upon special approval by the IABC Executive Committee and the director representing ethics on the Executive Board.

The first function should be to offer an IABC member service in assisting with general ethical questions related to the profession. The committee would not provide legal opinions. Opinions on questions would be solicited from an additional two accredited members and one member at random, and these would be factored into the review committee's summary opinion. Names of those requesting and giving opinions would be confidential.

The second function of the review committee would be the professional development of members on the subject of ethics, working in conjunction with IABC's professional development committee. Efforts should be made to inform and educate membership on matters of ethics, focusing on helping individuals develop ethical decision-making skills that are interdependent with IABC policy.

The third function should be to review and sanction violations of ethical conduct among members as they reflect on IABC and the communication profession. If a member's conduct is deemed by the director responsible for ethics to violate IABC's ethical code in a way that jeopardizes the credibility of the organization and profession, then the matter would first be discussed with the individual to determine the facts of the situation. Then, if circumstances warrant, the matter would be taken up by the ethics review committee. The individual's name would be kept confidential. In addition to the committee's deliberation, at least three additional opinions would be sought in any decision. Two opinions would be solicited at random from the pool of accredited members and one from a member-at-large. The IABC director representing ethics on the Executive Board would be an ex-officio member of the process.

Members of the ethics review committee would serve staggered, three-year consecutive terms to ensure internal consistency. They may serve more than one term but not consecutively. Members of the committee will be IABC accredited as a means of objective evidence that they have a working knowledge of communication ethics which meets the organization's standards of professionalism. Non-accredited members may be appointed upon special approval by the IABC Executive Committee and the director representing ethics on the Executive Board.

Sanctions

It is recognized that while the code may apply to communication professionals generally, sanctions would apply only to IABC members.

For a first violation, unless criminal activity is involved, the sanctions would be informative and educational. They would share concern over the situation, rendering opinions with the intent to help guide the member toward more professional performance.

A second violation for the same or related offense would bring a warning, again with the intent of information and education.

A third or subsequent violation could involve a further warning, or if the situation was flagrant without serious commitment of improvement, an alternative sanction of suspension for up to one year could be given. *Any decision of suspension or reinstatement must be reviewed and approved by the IABC Executive Committee and the executive board director responsible.*

Notes

Chapter One

1. John Paluszek, "Public Relations and Ethical Leadership: If Not Us, Who? If Not Now, When?", speech to the Public Relations Society of America, Westchester-Fairfield, N.Y. chapter, June 15, 1989, 6.
2. Paul Burton, *Corporate Public Relations* (New York: Reinhold, 1966), 6.
3. Mark P. McElreath, *Managing Systematic and Ethical Public Relations* (Dubuque, Iowa: Brown & Benchmark, 1993), 9.
4. Paul S. Forbes, "Revitalizing Business Ethics," *PRSA White Paper* (January 1989), 1.
5. Lyle F. Schoenfeldt et al., "The Teaching of Business Ethics: A Survey of AACSB Member Schools," *Journal of Business Ethics* (1991), 237.
6. Kenneth Labich, "The New Crisis in Business Ethics," *Fortune* (April 20, 1992), 168.
7. *Institute for Crisis Management Newsletter* (February 1993), 1.
8. Ibid., 3.
9. Forbes, "Revitalizing Business Ethics," 1.
10. John and Fritzsche Tsalikis, "Business Ethics: A Literature Review with a Focus on Marketing Ethics," *Journal of Business Ethics* (September 1989), 695.
11. John F. Budd, "A Pragmatic Examination of Ethical Dilemmas in Public Relations," IPRA Gold Paper No. 8 (1991), 9.
12. Michael Winkleman, "Soul Searching," *Public Relations Journal* (October 1987), 32.
13. E.W. Brody, "We Must Act Now to Redeem PR's Reputation," *Public Relations Quarterly* (Fall 1992), 44.
14. Cornelius B. Pratt, "Public Relations: The Empirical Research on Practitioner Ethics," *Journal of Business Ethics* (1991), 229.
15. Donald K. Wright, "Ethics Research in Public Relations: An Overview," *Public Relations Review* (Summer 1989), 1–67.
16. Gay Wakefield, "Trouble, Trouble, Trouble . . ." *PR Update* (April 1993), 4.

17. Jim Pritchett, "If Image Is Linked to Reputation, and Reputation to Increased Use, Shouldn't We Do Something About Ours?" *Public Relations Quarterly* (Fall 1992), 45.

18. Winkleman, "Soul Searching," 29.

19. Daniel J. Edelman, "Ethical Behavior Is Key to Field's Future," *Public Relations Journal* (November 1992), 31.

20. Brody, "We Must Act Now," 44.

21. Public Relations Society of America, "Report of Special Committee on Terminology" (April 11, 1987), 16, 25.

22. Ibid., 25.

23. Pritchett, "If Image Is Linked to Reputation," 47.

24. Todd Hunt and James E. Grunig, *Public Relations Techniques* (Fort Worth, Tex.: Harcourt Brace, 1994), 397.

25. Larry R. Judd, "Credibility, Public Relations and Social Responsibility," *Public Relations Review* (Summer 1989), 34.

26. S. Andrew Ostapski, "The Moral Audit," *B & E Review* (January-March 1992), 17.

27. Robert W. Kinkead and Dena Winokur, "How Public Relations Professionals Help CEOs Make the Right Moves," *Public Relations Journal* (October 1992), 19.

Kathy R. Fitzpatrick, "Who's in Charge: Balancing Public Relations and Legal Counsel in a Crisis," *Journal of Corporate Public Relations* (Winter 1993), 23.

28. John F. Steiner, "The Prospect of Ethical Advisors for Business Corporations," *Business and Society* (16), 5.

29. John D. Francis, "A Look Beneath the Bottom Line," *Public Relations Journal* (January 1990), 32.

30. Ibid., 16.

31. Ibid., 32.

32. Leonard Saffir with John Tarrant, *Power Public Relations* (Lincolnwood, Ill." NTC Business Books, 1992), 250.

33. Ibid., 251.

34. Patricia Houlihan Parsons, "Framework for Analysis of Conflicting Loyalties," *Public Relations Review* (Spring 1993), 51.

35. James Gaa, "A Game-Theoretic Analysis of Professional Rights and Responsibilities," *Journal of Business Ethics* (March 1990), 160.

36. John L. Carey, "Professional Ethics Are a Helpful Tool," *Public Relations Journal* (March 1957), 7.

37. Ibid.

38. Raymond Simon, *Public Relations: Concepts and Practices* (Columbus, Ohio: Grid Publishing, 1980), 394.

39. Wakefield, "Trouble, Trouble, Trouble ...", 4.

Chapter Two

1. Parsons, "Framework for Analysis," 53.

2. James E. Grunig and Jon White, "The Effect of Worldviews on Public Relations Theory and Practice," in *Excellence in Public Relations and Communication Management* (Hillsdale, N.J.: Lawrence Erlbaum Associates, 1992), 39.

3. Ibid., 40.

4. James E. Grunig and Larissa A. Grunig, "Models of Public Relations and Communication," in *Excellence in Public Relations and Communication Management* (Hillsdale, N.J.: Lawrence Erlbaum Associates, 1992), 308.

5. Thomas H. Bivins, "Public Relations, Professionalism, and the Public Interest," *Journal of Business Ethics* (1993), 118.

6. Ibid., 120–121.

7. Ibid., 126.

8. Ibid.

9. Clifford G. Christians, Kim B. Rotzoll, and Mark Fackler, *Media Ethics* (White Plains, N.Y.: Longman, 1991), 24.

10. Ibid., 24–25.

11. Gene Laczniak, "Business Ethics: A Manager's Primer," *Business* (33, 1983), 8.

12. Michael Josephson, "Teaching Ethical Decision Making and Principled Reasoning," in *Business Ethics* (Annual Editions 1993–1994) (Guilford, Conn.: Dushkin Publishing Group, 1993), 15.

13. Ibid.

14. *New World Dictionary* 2nd college ed. (Cleveland: William Collins Publishers, 1979), 732.

15. Melvin L. Sharpe, "Public Relations = Ethical Social Behavior," *PR Update* (April 1993), 3.

16. Robert Fulghum, *All I Really Need to Know I Learned in Kindergarten* (New York: Ivy Books, 1988), 4.

17. Daniel Brudney, "Two Links of Law and Morality," *Ethics* (January 1993), 280.

18. Verne E. Henderson, "The Ethical Side of Enterprise," *Sloan Management Review* (Spring 1982), 40.

19. Josephson, "Teaching Ethical Decision Making," 17.

20. Pratt, "Public Relations: The Empirical Research," 230.

21. Richard L. Johannesen, *Ethics in Human Communication* 3rd ed. (Prospect Heights, Ill.: Waveland, 1990), 170.

22. Rosalee A. Roberts, "Report to the PRSA Assembly Task Force on the Study of Ethical Issues" (November 13, 1993), 4.

23. Schoenfeldt, "The Teaching of Business Ethics," 237.

24. Winkleman, "Soul Searching," 30.

25. Ibid.

26. Karin Ireland, "The Ethics Game," *Personnel Journal* (March 1991), 72.

Randy N. Myers, "At Martin Marietta, This Board Game Is Lesson in Ethics," *Wall Street Journal* (September 25, 1992).

27. Ireland, "The Ethics Game," 75.

28. Ronald R. Sims, "The Challenge of Ethical Behavior in Organizations," *Journal of Business Ethics* (1992), 506.

29. Ibid., 510.

30. Ibid.

31. Ireland, "The Ethics Game," 72.

32. Fraser P. Seitel, *The Practice of Public Relations* 4th ed. (Columbus, Ohio: Merrill Publishing, 1989), 104.

33. Kinkead and Winokur, "How Public Relations Professionals Help CEOs," 20.

Chapter Three

1. *New World Dictionary*, 481.

2. McElreath, *Managing Systematic*, 320.

3. Thomas I. White, *Right and Wrong: A Brief Guide to Understanding Ethics* (Englewood Cliffs, N.J.: Prentice-Hall, 1988), 44.

4. McElreath, *Managing Systematic*, 323.

5. Karen Lebacqz, *Six Theories of Justice: Perspectives from Philosophical and Theological Ethics* (Minneapolis: Augsburg Publishing House, 1986), 15.

6. White, *Right and Wrong*, 51.

7. Ibid., 54.

8. Christians, Rotzoll, and Fackler, *Media Ethics*, 15.

9. White, *Right and Wrong*, 57.

10. Ibid., 65.

11. McElreath, *Managing Systematic*, 391.

12. White, *Right and Wrong*, 71.

13. Ibid., 69.

14. Ibid., viii.

15. David L. Martinson, "Can We Really Teach Public Relations Students to Be Ethical Practitioners?" *PR Update* (April 1993), 5.

16. John A. Byrne, "Can Ethics Be Taught? Harvard Gives It the Old College Try," *Business Week* (April 6, 1992), 34.

17. Andrew Stark, "What's the Matter with Business Ethics?" *Harvard Business Review* (May-June 1993), 44.

18. Josephson, "Teaching Ethical Decision Making," 14.

19. Stark, "What's the Matter," 38.

20. Christians, Rotzoll, and Fackler, *Media Ethics*, 4.

21. Ibid.

22. Sims, "The Challenge of Ethical Behavior," 512.

23. Frank Navran, "The Big PLUS in Ethical Decision Making," in *Book of Proceedings, 5th Annual National Conference on Ethics in America, 1994*, 514.

24. Josephson, "Teaching Ethical Decision Making," 19.

Chapter Four

1. Labich, "The New Crisis in Business Ethics," 167.

2. John Paul Fraedrich, "Signs and Signals of Unethical Behavior," *Business Forum* (Spring 1992), 13.

3. Sims, "The Challenge of Ethical Behavior," 507.

4. Preston Townley, "Business Ethics: Commitment to Tough Decisions," speech before the 44th National Conference of the Public Relations Society of America (November 3, 1991), 210.

5. Banks McDowell, "The Professional's Dilemma: Choosing Between Service and Success," *Business and Professional Ethics Journal* (9, 1/2), 35.

6. Ibid., 36.
Carey, "Professional Ethics Are a Helpful Tool," 7.

7. McDowell, "The Professional's Dilemma," 36.

8. Counselors Academy of the Public Relations Society of America, "Issues and Trends in the 1990s" (March 1992), 53.

9. Ibid.

10. Public Relations Society of America news release (February 14, 1977).

11. Budd, "A Pragmatic Examination," 14.

12. Ibid.

13. Ibid.

14. Burt Schorr, "Public Relations Society Draws Ire of FTC Over Code," *Wall Street Journal* (March 4, 1977), 1.

15. Frank Jefkins, *Public Relations* (London: Pitman Publishing, 1988), 12.

16. Saffir, *Power Public Relations*, 251.

17. Dean Kruckeberg, "Ethical Decision Making in Public Relations," *International Public Relations Review* (15 [4], 1992), 34.

18. Edelman, "Ethical Behavior Is Key," 32.

19. Jeffrey Goodell, "What Hill & Knowlton Can Do for You (And What It Couldn't Do for Itself)," *New York Times Magazine* (September 9, 1990), 74.

20. Ibid.

21. Ibid.

Arthur E. Rowse, "Flacking for the Emir," *The Progressive* (May 1991), 20.

22. Thomas H. Bivins, "A Systems Model for Ethical Decision Making in Public Relations," *Public Relations Review* (Winter 1992), 368.

John P. Ferre, "Ethical Public Relations: Pro Bono Work Among PRSA Members," *Public Relations Review* (Spring 1993), 60.

23. Kruckeberg, "Ethical Decision Making," 35.

24. Ibid.

25. Ibid.

Pratt, "Public Relations: The Empirical Research," 231.

26. John W. Hill, *The Making of a Public Relations Man* (New York: Van Rees Press, 1963), 139.

27. Edelman, "Ethical Behavior Is Key," 31.

28. David A. Haberman and Harry A. Dolphin, *Public Relations: The Necessary Art* (Ames, Iowa: Iowa State University Press, 1988), 404.

29. Ibid., 405.

30. Pamela Sebastian, "Non-Profit Groups Seek Ethics Standard," *Wall Street Journal* (October 30, 1992), A 7.

31. Adam Zagorin, "Remember," *Time* (August 16, 1993), 36.

32. Ellen Graham, "Sprawling Bureaucracy Eats Up Most Profits of Girl Scout Cookies," *Wall Street Journal* (May 13, 1993), 1.

33. Rayna Skolnik, "Rebuilding Trust: Nonprofits Act To Boost Reputations," *Public Relations Journal* (September 1993), 29.

34. Ibid., 32.

35. Paul F. Buller et al., "The Challenge of Global Ethics," *Journal of Business Ethics* (October 1991), 767.

36. Joyce Wouters, *International Public Relations* (New York: Amacom, 1991), 133.

37. "Corrupt Practices of Foreign Lands Impact PR, Press," *O'Dwyer's PR Services* (December 1993), 1.

38. James A. Jaksa and Michael S. Pritchard, *Communication Ethics: Methods of Analysis* 2nd ed. (Belmont, Mass.: Wadsworth, 1994), 18.

39. Ibid., 19.

40. Kent Hodgson, "Adapting Ethical Decisions to a Global Marketplace," *Management Review* (May 1992), 57.

41. Wouters, *International Public Relations*, 133.

42. Andrew W. Singer, "Ethics: Are Standards Lower Overseas?" *Across the Board* (September 1991), 34.

43. Jere W. Morehead et al., "Complying with the Amended Foreign Corrupt Practices Act," *Risk Management* (April 1990), 77.

44. Singer, "Ethics: Are Standards Lower," 33.

45. Ibid., 34.

46. Dean Kruckeberg, "The Need for an International Code of Ethics," *Public Relations Review* (Summer 1989), 13.

47. Jefkins, *Public Relations*, 29.

Chapter Five

1. Marvin N. Olasky, "Ministers or Panderers: Issues Raised by the Public Relations Society Code of Standards," *Journal of Mass Media Ethics* (Fall-Winter 1985), 44.

2. Ibid., 45

3. Lee W. Baker, *The Credibility Factor: Putting Ethics to Work in Public Relations* (Homewood, Ill.: Business One Irwin, 1993), 195.

4. David R. Drobis, "Duty to Inquire Benefits Organizations," *Public Relations Journal* (July 1993), 31.

5. Ibid., 3.

6. Ibid., 31.

7. Charles S. Steinberg, *The Mass Communicators* (New York: Harper & Brothers, 1958), 356.

8. Clifford G. Christians, John P. Ferre, and Mark Fackler, *Good News: Social Ethics and the Press* (New York: Oxford University Press, 1993), 181.

9. Todd Hunt and James E. Grunig, *Public Relations Techniques* (Fort Worth, Tex.: Harcourt Brace, 1994), 104.

10. "Disinformation Not Justified in Corporate World," *Public Relations Journal* (February 1992), 97.

Chapter Six

1. John L. Hulteng, *Playing It Straight* (Chester, Conn.: Globe Pequot Press, 1981), 78.

2. Ibid., 86.

3. Mary Anne Ramer, "A PR Practitioner's Memo to Journalists," *Editor & Publisher* (October 10, 1992), 64.

4. H. Eugene Goodwin, *Groping for Ethics in Journalism* (Ames, Iowa: Iowa State University Press, 1987), 100.

5. Bruce M. Swain, *Reporters' Ethics* (Ames, Iowa: Iowa State University Press, 1978), 74.

6. Hulteng, *Playing It Straight*, 82.

7. Ibid., 28.

8. Andrew Radolf, "Junket Journalism?" *Editor & Publisher* (October 18, 1986), 16.

9. Ibid.

10. George Garneau, "Ethics Debate Reprised," *Editor & Publisher* (October 19, 1991), 14.

11. Jeff Blyskal and Marie Blyskal, *PR: How the Public Relations Industry Writes the News* (New York: William Morrow, 1985), 46.

12. Ron Cantera, " 'Flacks' vs. 'Hacks'," *Editor & Publisher* (January 13, 1990), 27.

13. Blyskal and Blyskal, *PR*, 80

14. Bruce Porter, "The Scanlon Spin," *Columbia Journalism Review* (September-October 1989), 53.

15. Carole Howard and Wilma Mathews, *On Deadline: Managing Media Relations* (Prospect Heights, Ill.: Waveland Press, 1985), 99.

16. Judy VanSlyke Turk, "Information Subsidies and Media Content," *Journalism Monographs* (December 1986), 26.

17. Craig Aronoff, "Credibility of Public Relations for Journalists," *Public Relations Review* (Fall 1975), 55.

18. Dennis W. Jeffers, "Performance Expectations as a Measure of Relative Status of News and PR People," *Journalism Quarterly* (Summer 1977), 306.

19. Dave Berkman, "The Rush to PR," *Quill* (April 1992), 32.

Chapter Seven

1. Stanley Kelley, Jr., *Professional Public Relations and Political Power* (Baltimore: Johns Hopkins University Press, 1966), 3.

2. Sidney Blumenthal, *The Permanent Campaign* (Boston: Beacon Press, 1980), 1.

3. Rita Kirk Whillock, *Political Empiricism* (New York: Praeger, 1991), 199.

4. Joseph Napolitan, *The Election Game and How to Win It* (Garden City, N.Y.: Doubleday, 1972), 2.

5. Jarol Manheim, *All of the People, All the Time* (Armonk, N.Y.: M.E. Sharpe, 1991), 239.

6. Blumenthal, *The Permanent Campaign*, 20.

7. Ibid.

8. Ronald W. Clark, *Freud: The Man and the Cause* (New York: Random House, 1980), 278.

9. Blumenthal, *The Permanent Campaign*, 24.

10. Gil Troy, *See How They Ran* (New York: The Free Press, 1991), 136.

11. Ibid., 142.

12. Greg Mitchell, *The Campaign of the Century* (New York: Random House, 1992), 571.

13. Ibid., 570.

14. Napolitan, *The Election Game*, 11.

15. Kelley, *Professional Public Relations and Political Power*, 232.

16. Whillock, *Political Empiricism*, 199.

17. Blumenthal, *The Permanent Campaign*, 4.

18. Roger Simon, *Road Show* (New York: Farrar Straus Giroux, 1990), 167.

19. Philip Seib, *Campaigns and Conscience: The Ethics of Political Journalism* (New York: Praeger, 1994), 66.

20. Dave McNeely, "The Spread of Spin Doctors," *Dallas Morning News* (October 27, 1993), A 21.

21. Joel Brinkley, "Cultivating the Grass Roots to Reap Legislative Benefits," *New York Times* (November 1, 1993), A 1.

22. Kelley, *Professional Public Relations and Political Power*, 101.

23. Brinkley, "Cultivating Grass Roots," A 1.

24. Ibid., A 14.

25. Phil Kuntz, "Lobby Bill Would Plug Holes But Depends on Good Will," *Congressional Quarterly Weekly Report* (January 22, 1994), 103.

26. Brinkley, "Cultivating Grass Roots," A 14.

27. Hedrick Smith, *The Power Game* (New York: Random House, 1988), 231.

28. Douglass Cater, *Power in Washington* (New York: Vintage, 1965), 205.

29. Ibid., 200.

30. Smith, *The Power Game*, 269.

31. John Martin, "The Plan to Sell the War," ABC News, "20/20" (January 17, 1992), 4–5).

32. John R. MacArthur, *Second Front: Censorship and Propaganda in the Gulf War* (New York: Hill and Wang, 1992), 58.

33. Thomas E. Eidson, "Letter to the Editor: PR Firm Had No Reason to Question Kuwaiti's Testimony," *New York Times* (January 19, 1992), A 18.

34. Martin, "The Plan to Sell the War," 5.

35. MacArthur, *Second Front*, 47.

36. Ibid., 238.

37. Michael Wines, "A New Maxim for Lobbyists: What You Know, Not Whom," *New York Times* (November 3, 1993), A 1.

38. Ibid., C 22.

39. Scott M. Cutlip and Allen H. Center, *Effective Public Relations* 5th ed. (Englewood Cliffs, N.J.: Prentice-Hall, 1978), 499.

40. Ibid., 504.

41. Blyskal and Blyskal, *PR*, 189.

42. Cutlip and Center, *Effective Public Relations*, 512.

43. Blyskal and Blyskal, *PR*, 198.

44. Susan B. Garland and Lee Walczak, "It's the Money, Stupid," *Business Week* (November 15, 1993), 163.

45. Carole Gorney, "Litigation Journalism Is a Scourge," *New York Times* (February 28, 1993), 6/Z1.

46. Richard A. Oppel, Jr., "American's Spin Squad Woos Public," *Dallas Morning News* (August 8, 1993), 1 H.

47. Leonard Saffir with John Tarrant, *Power Public Relations* (Lincolnwood, Ill.: NTC Business Books, 1992), 117.

Chapter Eight

1. Mark L. Mitchell, "The Impact of External Parties on Brand-Name Capital: The 1982 Tylenol Poisonings and Subsequent Cases," *Economic Inquiry* (October 1989), 601.

2. Ibid., 603.

3. Hunt and Grunig, *Public Relations Techniques*, 185.

4. Laurence Barton, *Crisis in Organizations* (Cincinnati: South-Western Publishing, 1993), 84.

5. "Tylenol's 'Miracle' Comeback," *Time* (October 17, 1983), 67.

6. Bill Powell, "The Tylenol Rescue," *Newsweek* (March 3, 1986), 52.

7. Ibid., 53.

8. Ibid., 52.

9. "Johnson & Johnson's Class Act," *Business Week* (March 3, 1986), 134.

10. Andrea Rothman, "Who's That Screaming at Exxon? Not the Environmentalists," *Business Week* (May 1, 1989), 31.

11. Barbara Rudolph, "Nowhere to Run or Hide," *Time* (May 29, 1989), 69.

12. Alex Stanton, "Crises '89: On the Home Front," *Public Relations Journal* (September 1989), 16.

13. E. Bruce Harrison with Tom Prugh, "Assessing the Damage: Practitioner Perspectives on the Valdez," *Public Relations Journal* (October 1989), 40.

14. John Holusha, "Exxon's Public Relations Problem," *New York Times* (April 20, 1989), 1 B.

15. "In Ten Years You'll See 'Nothing'," *Fortune* (May 8, 1989), 54.

16. Robert Bazell, "Potemkin Cleanup," *The New Republic* (September 18 & 25, 1989), 22.

17. "Exxon Oil Slick," *The Nation* (September 25, 1989), 299.

18. L.J. Campbell, "Alms from Exxon: Radio Net's Oily Dilemma," *Washington Journalism Review* (June 1989), 14.

19. "The Tanker Was Three-Quarters Full," *Time* (May 1, 1989), 41.

20. Harrison, "Assessing the Damage," 41.

21. Ibid.

22. Ibid., 42.

23. Blyskal and Blyskal, *PR*, 169.

24. Ibid.

25. Stanton, "Crises '89," 15.

26. Leonard Snyder, "An Anniversary Review and Critique: The Tylenol Crisis," *Public Relations Review* (Fall 1983), 24.

Chapter Nine

1. Hunt and Grunig, *Public Relations Techniques*, 395.

2. James E. Grunig, "Public Relations and International Affairs: Effects, Ethics and Responsibility," *Journal of International Affairs* (Summer 1993), 141.

3. Donald K. Wright, "Enforcement Dilemma: Voluntary Nature of Public Relations Codes," *Public Relations Review* (Spring 1993), 13.

4. Susan Fry Bovet, "The Burning Question of Ethics," *Public Relations Journal*, 24.

Bibliography

ABC News, "20/20." "The Plan to Sell the War." Transcript No. 1203, January 17, 1992.

Aronoff, Craig. "Credibility of Public Relations for Journalists." *Public Relations Review*, Fall 1975, 45.

Baker, Lee W. *The Credibility Factor: Putting Ethics to Work in Public Relations*. Homewood, Ill.: Business One Irwin, 1993.

Barton, Laurence. *Crisis in Organizations*. Cincinnati: South-Western Publishing, 1993.

Bazell, Robert. "Potemkin Cleanup." *The New Republic*, September 18 & 25, 1989, 22.

Berkman, Dave. "The Rush to PR." *Quill*, April 1992, 31.

Bivins, Thomas H. "Public Relations, Professionalism, and the Public Interest." *Journal of Business Ethics* 12, 1993, 117.

_____ . "A Systems Model for Ethical Decision Making in Public Relations." *Public Relations Review* 18 (4), Winter 1992, 365–383.

Blumenthal, Sidney. *The Permanent Campaign*. Boston: Beacon Press, 1980.

Blyskal, Jeff, and Blyskal, Marie. *PR: How the Public Relations Industry Writes the News*. New York: William Morrow, 1985.

Bok, Sissela. *Lying: Moral Choice in Public and Private Life*. New York: Pantheon, 1978.

Bovet, Susan Fry. "The Burning Question of Ethics." *Public Relations Journal*, November 1993, 24.

Brinkley, Joel. "Cultivating the Grass Roots to Reap Legislative Benefits." *New York Times*, November 1, 1993, A 1.

Brody, E.W. "We Must Act Now to Redeem PR's Reputation." *Public Relations Quarterly*, Fall 1992, 44.

Brody, E.W., ed. *New Technology and Public Relations*. Sarasota: The Institute for Public Relations Research and Education, 1991.

Brudney, Daniel. "Two Links of Law and Morality." *Ethics*, January 1993, 280.

Budd, John F. "A Pragmatic Examination of Ethical Dilemmas in Public Relations." IPRA Gold Paper No. 8, 1991.

Buller, Paul F. et al. "The Challenge of Global Ethics." *Journal of Business Ethics* 10 (10), October 1991, 767–775.

Burton, Paul. *Corporate Public Relations.* New York: Reinhold, 1966.

Byrne, John A. "Can Ethics Be Taught? Harvard Gives It the Old College Try." *Business Week*, April 6, 1992, 34.

Campbell, L.J. "Alms from Exxon: Radio Net's Oily Dilemma." *Washington Journalism Review*, June 1989, 14.

Canfield, Bertrand R. *Public Relations* 5th ed. Homewood, Ill.: Irwin, 1968.

Cantera, Ron. " 'Flacks' vs. 'Hacks'." *Editor & Publisher*, January 13, 1990, 48.

Cantor, Bill, and Burger, Chester. *Experts in Action: Inside Public Relations.* New York: Longman, 1984.

Carey, John L. "Professional Ethics Are a Helpful Tool." *Public Relations Journal*, March 1957, 7.

Cater, Douglass. *Power in Washington.* New York: Vintage, 1965.

Christians, Clifford G., Ferre, John P., and Fackler, Mark. *Good News: Social Ethics and the Press.* New York: Oxford University Press 1993.

Christians, Clifford G., Rotzoll, Kim B., and Fackler, Mark. *Media Ethics* 3rd ed. White Plains, N.Y.: Longman, 1991.

Clark, Ronald W. *Freud: The Man and the Cause.* New York: Random House, 1980.

Cooper, Robert W., and Frank, Garry L. "Professionals in Business: Where Do They Look for Help in Dealing with Ethical Issues?" *Business and Professional Ethics Journal*, Vol. 11, No. 2, 40.

"Corrupt Practices of Foreign Lands Impact PR, Press." *O'Dwyer's PR Services*, December 1993, 1.

Counselors Academy of the Public Relations Society of America. "Issues and Trends in the 1990s." March 1992.

Cutlip, Scott M., and Center, Allen H. *Effective Public Relations* 5th ed. Englewood Cliffs, N.J.: Prentice-Hall, 1978.

Davidson, Spencer. "A Replay of the Tylenol Scare." *Time*, February 24, 1986, 22.

Davis, Michael. "Working with Your Company's Code of Ethics." *Management Solutions*, June 1988, 5.

Decker, Francis K. "PRSA's Code: How the Practitioner and Public Are Protected." *Public Relations Journal*, March 1967, 26.

Dennis, Everette E., and Merrill, John C. *Media Debates.* New York: Longman, 1991.

"Disinformation Not Justified in Corporate World." *Public Relations Journal*, February 1992, 97.

Drobis, David R. "Duty to Inquire Benefits Organizations." *Public Relations Journal*, July 1993, 32.

Edelman, Daniel J. "Ethical Behavior Is Key to Field's Future." *Public Relations Journal*, November 1992, 32.

Eidson, Thomas E. "Letter to the Editor: PR Firm Had No Reason to Question Kuwaiti's Testimony." *New York Times*, January 19, 1992, A 16.

"Ethics Code for Business Partners." *Ethical Management*, January 1994, 5.

"Exxon Oil Slick." *The Nation*. September 25, 1989, 299.

Ferre, John P. "Ethical Public Relations: Pro Bono Work Among PRSA Members." *Public Relations Review* 19 (1), Spring 1993, 59.

Fitzpatrick, Kathy R. "Who's in Charge: Balancing Public Relations and Legal Counsel in a Crisis." *Journal of Corporate Public Relations*, Winter 1993, 21.

Forbes, Paul S. "Revitalizing Business Ethics." *PRSA White Paper*, January 1989.

Fraedrich, John Paul. "Signs and Signals of Unethical Behavior." *Business Forum*, Spring 1992, 13.

Francis, John D. "A Look Beneath the Bottom Line." *Public Relations Journal*, January 1990, 16.

Frederick, William C. "The Moral Authority of Transnational Corporate Codes." *Journal of Business Ethics* 10 (3), March 1991, 165.

Fulghum, Robert. *All I Really Need to Know I Learned in Kindergarten*. New York: Ivy Books, 1988.

Gaa, James. "A Game-Theoretic Analysis of Professional Rights and Responsibilities." *Journal of Business Ethics* 9 (3), March 1990, 159.

Garland, Susan B., and Walczak, Lee. "It's the Money, Stupid." *Business Week*, November 15, 1993, 163.

Garneau, George. "Ethics Debate Reprised." *Editor & Publisher*, October 19, 1991, 14.

Goldman, Eric F. *Two-Way Street: The Emergence of Public Relations Counsel*. Boston: Bellman, 1948.

Goodell, Jeffrey. "What Hill & Knowlton Can Do for You (And What It Couldn't Do for Itself)." *New York Times Magazine*, September 9, 1990, 44.

Goodwin, H. Eugene. *Groping for Ethics in Journalism* 2nd ed. Ames, Iowa: Iowa State University Press, 1987.

Gorney, Carole. "Litigation Journalism Is a Scourge." *New York Times*, February 28, 1993, 6/Z1.

Graham, Ellen. "Sprawling Bureaucracy Eats Up Most Profits of Girl Scout Cookies." *Wall Street Journal*, May 13, 1993, 1.

Grunig, James E. "Public Relations and International Affairs: Effects, Ethics and Responsibility." *Journal of International Affairs*, Vol. 47, No. 1, Summer 1993, 137.

Grunig, James E., and Grunig, Larissa A. "Models of Public Relations and Communication." In *Excellence in Public Relations and Communication Management*. Hillsdale, N.J.: Lawrence Erlbaum Associates, 1992, 285.

Grunig, James E., and White, Jon. "The Effect of Worldviews on Public Relations Theory and Practice." In *Excellence in Public Relations and Communication Management*. Hillsdale, N.J.: Lawrence Erlbaum Associates, 1992, 31.

Haberman, David A., and Dolphin, Harry A. *Public Relations: The Necessary Art*. Ames, Iowa: Iowa State University Press, 1988.

Harrison, E. Bruce, with Tom Prugh. "Assessing the Damage: Practitioner Perspectives on the Valdez." *Public Relations Journal*, October 1989, 40.

Henderson, Verne E. "The Ethical Side of Enterprise." *Sloan Management Review*, Spring 1982, 37.

Hill, John W. *The Making of a Public Relations Man*. New York: Van Rees Press, 1963.

Hodgson, Kent. "Adapting Ethical Decisions to a Global Marketplace." *Management Review*, May 1992, 53.

Holusha, John. "Exxon's Public Relations Problem." *New York Times*, April 20, 1989, 1 B.

Howard, Carole, and Mathews, Wilma. *On Deadline: Managing Media Relations*. Prospect Heights, Ill.: Waveland, 1985.

Hulteng, John L. *Playing It Straight*. Chester, Conn.: Globe Pequot Press, 1981.

Hunt, Todd, and Grunig, James E. *Public Relations Techniques*. Fort Worth, Tex.: Harcourt Brace, 1994.

Hunt, Todd, and Tirpok, Andrew. "Universal Ethics Code: An Idea Whose Time Has Come." *Public Relations Review*, Spring 1993, 1.

Institute for Crisis Management Newsletter, February 1993, 1.

"In Ten Years You'll See 'Nothing'." *Fortune*, May 8, 1989, 50.

Ireland, Karin. "The Ethics Game." *Personnel Journal*, March 1991, 72.

Jaksa, James A., and Pritchard, Michael S. *Communication Ethics: Methods of Analysis* 2nd ed. Belmont, Mass.; Wadsworth, 1994.

Jeffers, Dennis W. "Performance Expectations as a Measure of Relative Status of News and PR People." *Journalism Quarterly*, Summer 1977, 299.

Jefkins, Frank. *Public Relations*. London: Pitman Publishing, 1988.

Johannesen, Richard L. *Ethics in Human Communication* 3rd ed. Prospect Heights, Ill.: Waveland, 1990.

"Johnson & Johnson's Class Act." *Business Week*, March 3, 1986, 134.

Josephson, Michael. "Teaching Ethical Decision Making and Principled Reasoning." In *Business Ethics* (Annual Editions 1993–1994). Guilford, Conn.: Dushkin Publishing Group, 1993, 13.

Judd, Larry R. "Credibility, Public Relations and Social Responsibility." *Public Relations Review*, Summer 1989, 34.

Karp, H.B., and Abramms, Bob. "Doing the Right Thing." *Training and Development*, August 1992, 37.

Katzman, Jodi B. "What's the Role of Public Relations?" *Public Relations Journal*, April 1993, 11.

Kelley, Stanley, Jr. *Professional Public Relations and Political Power*. Baltimore: Johns Hopkins, 1966.

Kinkead, Robert W., and Winokur, Dena. "How Public Relations Professionals Help CEOs Make the Right Moves." *Public Relations Journal*, October 1992, 20.

Kruckeberg, Dean. "Ethical Decision-Making in Public Relations." *International Public Relations Review* 15 (4), 1992, 32.

____ . "The Need for an International Code of Ethics." *Public Relations Review*, Summer 1989, 6.

____ . "Universal Ethics Code: Both Possible and Feasible." *Public Relations Review* 19 (1), Spring 1993, 21.

Kuntz, Phil. "Lobby Bill Would Plug Holes But Depends on Good Will." *Congressional Quarterly Weekly Report*, January 22, 1994, 103.

Labich, Kenneth. "The New Crisis in Business Ethics." *Fortune*, April 20, 1992, 167.

Laczniak, Gene. "Business Ethics: A Manager's Primer." *Business* 33, 1983, 23.

Lebacqz, Karen. *Six Theories of Justice: Perspectives from Philosophical and Theological Ethics*. Minneapolis: Augsburg Publishing House, 1986.

MacArthur, John R. "Remember Nayirah, Witness for Kuwait?" *New York Times*, January 6, 1992, A 17.

MacArthur, John R. *Second Front: Censorship and Propaganda in the Gulf War*. New York: Hill and Wang, 1992.

"Management Focus." *The Economist*, June 5, 1993, 71.

Manheim, Jarol. *All of the People All the Time*. Armonk, N.Y.: M.E. Sharpe, 1991.

Martin, John. "The Plan to Sell the War." ABC News, "20/20," January 17, 1992.

Martinson, David L. "Can We Really Teach Public Relations Students to Be Ethical Practitioners?" *PR Update*, April 1993, 5.

McDowell, Banks. "The Professional's Dilemma: Choosing Between Service and Success." *Business and Professional Ethics Journal* 9 (1/2), 35.

McElreath, Mark P. *Managing Systematic and Ethical Public Relations*. Dubuque, Iowa: Brown & Benchmark, 1993.

McNeely, Dave. "The Spread of Spin Doctors." *Dallas Morning News*, October 27, 1993, A 21.

Mintz, Morton. *At Any Cost*. New York: Pantheon, 1985.

Mitchell, Greg. *The Campaign of the Century*. New York: Random House, 1992.

Mitchell, Mark L. "The Impact of External Parties on Brand-Name Capital: The 1982 Tylenol Poisonings and Subsequent Cases." *Economic Inquiry*, XXVII, October 1989, 619.

Montagna, Catherine. "Nonprofits Survive Scandals, Budget Crunch." *Public Relations Journal*, May 1993, 8.

Morehead, Jere W. et al. "Complying With the Amended Foreign Corrupt Practices Act." *Risk Management* 37:4, April 1990, 76–82.

Myers, Randy N. "At Martin Marietta, This Board Game Is Lesson in Ethics." *Wall Street Journal*, September 25, 1992.

Napolitan, Joseph. *The Election Game and How to Win It*. Garden City, N.Y.: Doubleday, 1972.

Navran, Frank. "The Big PLUS in Ethical Decision Making." In *Book of Proceedings, 5th Annual National Conference on Ethics in America, 1994*, 509.

New World Dictionary 2nd college ed. Cleveland: William Collins Publishers, 1979.

Newstrom, John W., and Ruch, William A. "The Ethics of Management and the Management of Ethics." *MSU Business Topics*, Winter 1975, 29.

Olasky, Marvin N. "Ministers or Panderers: Issues Raised by the Public Relations Society Code of Standards." *Journal of Mass Media Ethics*, Fall-Winter 1985, 43.

Oppel, Richard A., Jr. "American's Spin Squad Woos Public." *Dallas Morning News*, August 8, 1993, 1 H.

Ostapski, S. Andrew. "The Moral Audit." *B & E Review*, January-March 1992, 17.

Paluszek, John. "Public Relations and Ethical Leadership: If Not Us, Who? If Not Now, When?" Speech to the Public Relations Society of America, Westchester-Fairfield chapter, Rye, N.Y., June 15, 1989.

Parsons, Patricia Houlihan. "Framework for Analysis of Conflicting Loyalties." *Public Relations Review* 19 (1), Spring 1993, 49.

Porter, Bruce. "The Scanlon Spin." *Columbia Journalism Review*, September-October 1989, 49.

Powell, Bill. "The Tylenol Rescue." *Newsweek*, March 3, 1986, 52.

Pratt, Cornelius B. "PRSA Members' Perceptions of Public Relations Ethics." *Public Relations Review*, Summer 1991, 145.

——— . "Public Relations: The Empirical Research on Practitioner Ethics." *Journal of Business Ethics* 10, 1991, 229.

Pritchett, Jim. "If Image Is Linked to Reputation, and Reputation to Increased Use, Shouldn't We Do Something About Ours?" *Public Relations Quarterly*, Fall 1992, 45.

Public Relations Society of America news release, February 14, 1977.

Public Relations Society of America, "Report of Special Committee on Terminology," April 11, 1987.

Purdy, Kathleen. "Editor's Reflections." *Ethical Management*, January 1994, 8.

Radolf, Andrew. "Junket Journalism?" *Editor & Publisher*, October 18, 1986, 16.

Raiborn, Cecily A., and Payne, Dinah. "Corporate Codes of Conduct: A Collective Conscience and Continuum." *Journal of Business Ethics*, 1990, 879.

Ramer, Mary Anne. "A PR Practitioner's Memo to Journalists." *Editor & Publisher*, October 10, 1992, 64.

Roberts, Rosalee A. "Report to the PRSA Assembly Task Force on the Study of Ethical Issues." November 13, 1993, 4.

Rothman, Andrea. "Who's That Screaming at Exxon? Not the Environmentalists." *Business Week*, May 1, 1989, 31.

Rotzoll, Kim, and Christians, Clifford. "Advertising Agency Practitioners' Perceptions of Ethical Decisions." *Journalism Quarterly*, August 1980, 425.

Rowse, Arthur E. "Flacking for the Emir." *The Progressive*, May 1991, 20.

Rudolph, Barbara. "Nowhere to Run or Hide." *Time*, May 29, 1989, 69.

Saffir, Leonard, with Tarrant, John. *Power Public Relations*. Lincolnwood, Ill.: NTC Business Books, 1992.

Schmertz, Herb, with Novak, William. *Good-bye to the Low Profile*. Boston: Little, Brown, 1986.

Schoenfeldt, Lyle F. et al. "The Teaching of Business Ethics: A Survey of AACSB Member Schools." *Journal of Business Ethics*, 1991, 237.

Schorr, Burt. "Public Relations Society Draws Ire of FTC Over Code." *Wall Street Journal*, March 4, 1977, 1.

Sebastian, Pamela. "Nonprofit Groups Seek Ethics Standard." *Wall Street Journal*, October 30, 1992, A 7.

Seib, Philip. *Campaigns and Conscience: The Ethics of Political Journalism*. New York: Praeger, 1994.

Seitel, Fraser P. *The Practice of Public Relations* 4th ed. Columbus, Ohio: Merrill Publishing, 1989.

Shamir, Jacob et al. "Individual Differences in Ethical Values of Public Relations Practitioners." *Journalism Quarterly* 67, Winter 1990, 956.

Sharpe, Melvin L. "Public Relations = Ethical Social Behavior." *PR Update*, April 1993, 3.

Simon, Raymond, ed. *Perspectives in Public Relations*. Norman, Okla.: University of Oklahoma Press, 1966.

Simon, Raymond. *Public Relations: Concepts and Practices*. Columbus, Ohio: Grid Publishing, 1980.

Simon, Roger. *Road Show*. New York: Farrar Straus Giroux, 1990.

Sims, Ronald R. "The Challenge of Ethical Behavior in Organizations." *Journal of Business Ethics* 11, 1992, 505.

Singer, Andrew W. "Can a Company Be Too Ethical?" *Across the Board*, April 1993, 17.

_____ . "Ethics: Are Standards Lower Overseas?" *Across the Board*, September 1991, 31.

Skolnik, Rayna. "Rebuilding Trust: Nonprofits Act to Boost Reputations." *Public Relations Journal*, September 1993, 29.

Smith, Hedrick. *The Power Game*. New York: Random House, 1988.

Snyder, Leonard. "An Anniversary Review and Critique: The Tylenol Crisis." *Public Relations Review*, Fall 1983, 24.

Stanton, Alex. "Crises '89: On the Home Front." *Public Relations Journal*, September 1989, 15.

Stark, Andrew. "What's the Matter with Business Ethics?" *Harvard Business Review*, May-June 1993.

Steinberg, Charles S. *The Mass Communicators*. New York: Harper & Brothers, 1958.

Steiner, John F. "The Prospect of Ethical Advisors for Business Corporations." *Business and Society* 16, 5.

Stephenson, D.R. "Internal PR Efforts Further Corporate Responsibility: A Report from Dow Canada." *Public Relations Quarterly*, Summer 1983, 7.

Swain, Bruce M. *Reporters' Ethics*. Ames, Iowa: Iowa State University Press, 1978.

"The Tanker Was Three-Quarters Full." *Time*, May 1, 1989, 41.

Towers, Alan. "Reputation Management: Path to Ascendancy." *Public Relations Journal*, January 1993, 25.

Townley, Preston. "Business Ethics: Commitment to Tough Decisions." Speech before the 44th National Conference of the Public Relations Society of America, Phoenix, Ariz., November 3, 1991.

Troy, Gil. *See How They Ran*. New York: The Free Press, 1991.

Tsalikis, John and Fritzsche. "Business Ethics: A Literature Review with a Focus on Marketing Ethics." *Journal of Business Ethics* 8 (9), September 1989, 695.

Turk, Judy VanSlyke. "Information Subsidies and Media Content." *Journalism Monographs*, December 1986.

"Tylenol's 'Miracle' Comeback." *Time*, October 17, 1983, 67.

Wakefield, Gay. "Trouble, Trouble, Trouble . . ." *PR Update*, April 1993, 4.

Whilock, Rita Kirk. *Political Empiricism*. New York: Praeger, 1991.

White, Thomas I. *Right and Wrong: A Brief Guide to Understanding Ethics*. Englewood Cliffs, N.J.: Prentice-Hall, 1988.

Wines, Michael. "A New Maxim for Lobbyists: What You Know, Not Whom." *New York Times*, November 3, 1993, A 1.

Winkleman, Michael. "Soul Searching." *Public Relations Journal*, October 1987, 28.

Wohlforth, Charles P. "Black Gold." *The New Republic*, September 18 & 25, 1989, 20.

Wouters, Joyce. *International Public Relations*. New York: Amacom, 1991.

Wright, Donald K. "Enforcement Dilemma: Voluntary Nature of Public Relations Codes." *Public Relations Review*, Spring 1993, 13.

_____ . "Ethics in Public Relations." *Public Relations Journal*, December 1982, 12.

_____ . "Ethics Research in Public Relations: An Overview." *Public Relations Review*, Summer 1989, 1.

_____ . "Examining Ethical and Moral Values of Public Relations People." *Public Relations Review*, Summer 1989, 19.

_____ . "Social Responsibility in Public Relations: A Multi-Step Theory." *Public Relations Review*, 2, 1976, 33.

Zagorin, Adam. "Remember." *Time*, August 16, 1993, 36.

Zey-Ferrell, Mary et al. "Predicting Unethical Behavior Among Marketing Practitioners." *Human Relations*, 32, No. 7, 1979, 557.

Index

Permissions

International Association of Business Communicators Code of Ethics is reprinted courtesy of the International Association of Business Communicators.

International Code of Ethics — Code of Athens is reprinted by permission of the International Public Relations Association.

International Public Relations Association Code of Conduct is reprinted by permission of the International Public Relations Association.

Public Relations Society of America Code of Professional Conduct is reprinted by permission of the Public Relations Society of America.

DATE DUE

| GAYLORD | | | PRINTED IN U.S.A. |